J. S. Bach

CALVIN R. STAPERT

For Ann,
with gratitude for forty-seven years
of blissful marriage

She is far more precious than jewels ...
Strength and dignity are her clothing ...
She opens her mouth with wisdom,
    and the teaching of kindness is on her tongue.
She looks well to the ways of her household ...
Her children rise up and call her blessed;
    her husband also, and he praises her:
'Many women have done excellently.
    but you surpass them all.'

FROM PROVERBS 31

Autograph manuscript of the D-minor Fugue
from Johann Sebastian Bach's *Well-Tempered
Clavier*, Part I, 1722.

J.S.BACH

LION

A Lion Book
an imprint of
Lion Hudson plc
Wilkinson House, Jordan Hill Road,
Oxford OX2 8DR, England
www.lionhudson.com
ISBN 978 0 7459 5286 4 (UK)
ISBN 978 0 8254 7924 3 (US)

Distributed by:
UK: Marston Book Services, PO Box 269, Abingdon, Oxon, OX14 4YN
USA: Trafalgar Square Publishing, 814 N. Franklin Street, Chicago, IL 60610
USA: Christian Market: Kregel Publications, PO Box 2607, Grand Rapids, MI, 49501

First edition 2009
10 9 8 7 6 5 4 3 2 1 0

Acknowledgments
Every effort has been made to trace and acknowledge copyright holders of all the quotations
included. We apologize for any errors or omissions that may remain, and would ask those
concerned to contact the publishers, who will ensure that full acknowledgment is made in
the future.
Scripture quotations taken from Bach's works are Calvin Stapert's translations of Luther's
German version. Other Scripture quotations are from The Holy Bible, English Standard
Version®, copyright © 2001 by Crossway Bibles, a publishing ministry of Good News
Publishers. Used by permission. All rights reserved.
Extract from *The New Bach Reader: A Life of Johann Sebastian Bach in Letters and Documents*,
edited by Hans T. David & Arthur Mendel, revised and enlarged by Christoph Wolff. Copyright
© 1966, 1945 by W. W. Norton & company, Inc. Copyright © 1927 by Mrs Hans T. David
and Arthur Mendel. Used by permission of W. W. Norton & Company, Inc.

The text paper used in this book has been made from wood
independently certified as having come from sustainable forests.

A catalogue record for this book is available from the British Library

Typeset in 10/14 Photina MT.

Printed in China.

Contents

PREFACE

With the exception of William Shakespeare, we probably know less about the private life of Johann Sebastian Bach than we do about that of any of the other supreme artistic figures of modern history. The documents bearing on his life that have survived, whether written by others or by Bach himself, are almost invariably 'official' in character: bills, receipts, letters of application, of appointment or resignation, letters of recommendation on behalf of pupils, complaints or reprimands to or from employers and other authorities, inspection reports on organs just built or about to be renovated. Not a single letter from Bach to any of his children, or to his first wife, Maria Barbara, or his second wife, Anna Magdalena, has survived; we may assume that not many were ever written.

So writes Bach scholar Robert Marshall regarding a significant lacuna in documentation that faces biographers of Bach. Of course, that has not deterred them from writing his biography. Despite the lacuna that Marshall laments, there is a mountain of documentation surrounding Bach, beginning with the biographical sketch in the Obituary written by Bach's son Carl Philipp Emanuel and one of his students. This, along with the 1802 biography by Johann Nikolaus Forkel, who got much of his information from Carl and his older brother, Wilhelm Friedemann, provide the starting point for all subsequent biographies of Bach. Both are sketchy and neither one is infallible. Nevertheless, they make a sturdy foundation upon which to build.

The biographer has lots of building material. There are the 'official' kinds of documents Marshall mentions. There is also a considerable amount of information about the people with whom Bach lived and worked, and the places – and more broadly the cultural environments – in which he lived and worked. What is largely missing is direct documentation of Bach's thoughts and feelings about people, events, politics, the big issues of life and death, or anything else. We do not have a steady stream of letters to family and friends, as we have for Mozart. We do not have journalistic music criticism from Bach's pen, as we have from Schumann's. We do not have effusive writings on philosophy, political theory, and aesthetics, as we have from Wagner. In other words, we have lots of information from outside of Bach, and seemingly little evidence from inside.

But we do have a Bible with commentary that Bach owned and marked with marginal notes and underlining. We also have an extensive body of texts that Bach set to music, a body of texts that express the theology of the Lutheran Reformation. In the present telling of the story of Bach's life, I have made the assumption that Bach's thinking, indeed his whole being, was shaped by that theology, a theology that he inherited from his ancestors and was given expression in the texts he set to music. G. K. Chesterton wrote in his biography of Chaucer, 'The greatest poets of the world have a certain serenity, because they have not bothered to invent a small philosophy, but have inherited a large philosophy.' Because I see that to be true of Bach, I do not hesitate to take the theology expressed in those texts – and even more particularly in those texts as they are expressed by Bach's music – as the key to Bach's own thoughts and feelings.

That theology was rooted in Luther's view of the Bible. *Sola Scriptura*, 'Scripture alone', was a watchword of the Reformation. Luther asserted that popes, Church Councils, and even the Church Fathers could and did err. Therefore only the Bible could be relied upon as the unconditional authority in all matters of faith and life. 'Hold to Scripture and the word of God', Luther said. 'There you will find truth and security – assurance and a faith that is complete, pure, sufficient, and enduring.' It is not surprising, then, that one of Luther's first major projects once the Reformation was under way, was to translate the Bible into German so that it could be read by all, not just by the educated who knew Latin. Neither is it surprising to find that the major part of his writings is exegetical lectures and sermons. His other writings also, in the words of Paul Althaus, 'are saturated with quotations from Scripture and are largely exegetical in character'.

Bach knew the Scripture-saturated writings of Luther well. He owned two sets of Luther's complete works. And the texts he set to music, like Luther's works, are saturated with scriptural quotations and allusions.

It would be hard to exaggerate the importance of the Bible in the Lutheran circles within which Bach lived and worked.

Sceptics, of course, can maintain that Bach's religion was simply 'pro forma'. If they want to believe that Bach set those Bible-saturated texts to music simply because it was his job, there is no 'proof' that can be offered to the contrary; but neither is there 'proof' for their belief. They can maintain, as some scholars have in recent years, that Bach had no 'intention' or 'heartfelt need' to proclaim the Christian faith, or that his music was a 'cloak' that hid (but subtly revealed) a more modern worldview. But such a view has to be maintained in the face of much that contributes to – and little, if anything, that points away from – a portrait of Bach as a devout Lutheran believer whose life and work were dedicated to the glory of his God and the well-being of his neighbour.

Bach's works are catalogued and numbered in the *Bach-Werke-Verzeichnis* (BWV). To help the reader locate scores or recordings of specific works, I have identified them throughout the book by their BWV number. Two things should be noted about these numbers. First, they are not chronological. The works are ordered by genre, and even within the generic groups, the numbers are not chronological. Second, the first pieces listed are the cantatas, so the BWV number and the cantata number are identical; for example Cantata 1 is BWV 1.

Most of the quotations from documentary sources have been taken from the translations in *The New Bach Reader* (Norton, 1998). Translations of other texts, unless otherwise indicated, are my own. Scriptural texts in the musical works themselves or in contemporary documents are from Luther's translation of the Bible. I have translated those texts directly from Luther's German, which accounts for their differences with familiar English translations of the Bible. When a scriptural passage is not quoted from some other source, I have used the English Standard Version.

Chapter 1
ROOTS AND EARLY CHILDHOOD: EISENACH (1685–1695)

I n January 1521 Pope Leo X excommunicated Martin Luther. In April, in an attempt to forestall further turmoil, Emperor Charles V summoned Luther to the city of Worms in southern Germany. Here he was to stand before an assembly, or diet, of the princes and electors of the Holy Roman Empire. Charles was hoping that Luther would recant. But at the conclusion of the Diet of Worms, in his famous 'Here I stand' speech, Luther refused to recant and Charles placed him under imperial ban. After the Diet, Luther was given safe conduct to return to Wittenberg, but while passing through the Thuringian Forest, he was abducted by horsemen of Frederick the Wise, elector of Saxony. They took him to the Wartburg Castle, an imposing structure at the top of a cliff 1,200 feet (366 metres) above the small town of Eisenach. The abduction, however, was a ruse to bring him into hiding for safekeeping. For nearly a year he was kept at the Wartburg as Junker Jörg (Knight George), disguised in knightly dress and a  newly grown beard. During his stay on his 'island of Patmos', as he called the Wartburg, he had time to consolidate his thoughts, carry on extensive correspondence, and translate the New Testament into German.

Eisenach and the Wartburg were familiar territory for Luther. When he was born his parents had only recently moved from Eisenach to Eisleben. Many of their relatives on both sides continued to live in Eisenach. When Martin was fifteen years old they sent him back to Eisenach to attend St George's Latin School. There he sang in the boy choir and finished preparatory studies for university. Later he preached at St George's Church

Martin Luther disguised as 'Knight George' in his hideout in Wartburg Castle, 1521/1522, where he translated the New Testament into German. Painted by his friend Lucas Cranich the Elder.

A view of Wartburg Castle located above the town of Eisenach. In 1999 the Wartburg was added to the Unesco World Heritage Site list.

on his way to and from the Diet of Worms and was in Eisenach on at least two more occasions. He referred to Eisenach as his 'dear city'.

The relationship was reciprocal: Luther was as dear to the citizens of Eisenach as the town was to him. They welcomed his theology, and it became firmly lodged in their minds for generations. His Large and Small Catechisms were central to the teaching in both church and school, and that teaching penetrated all the more deeply into the hearts of the people through the singing of chorales. Eisenach – indeed all of Thuringia – had the same love for music that Luther had. In 1685 the teacher, pastor, and hymn-writer Georg Michael Pfefferkorn wrote that in the villages of Thuringia even the

Part of the interior of St George's Church in Eisenach, where Bach was baptized.

farmers played and made all sorts of instruments – violins, violas da gamba, harpsichords, and zithers – and even in the most modest churches there was wonderful organ music. The 1698 Annals of Eisenach boasted: 'Our town was always celebrated for music – and what is the anagram of *Isenacum* [Eisenach] but *en musica* [look! music], or *canimus* [we sing]?'

Into Eisenach's musical and theological environment, a little more than a century and a half after Luther was brought to the Wartburg for refuge, a boy was born who would devote his enormous musical talent and energy to the glory of God in the service of the Lutheran Church. That boy was Johann Sebastian Bach, born 21 March 1685. He was baptized two days later in St George's Church, where Luther had preached, and as a young boy he attended the same Latin school Luther had attended. So not only was Sebastian (as we will call the young Bach to distinguish him from all the other Johanns) born into the heart of Luther country, but his earliest years were spent in close proximity to physical reminders of the great Reformer's presence, a presence that was still very strongly felt. As James R. Gaines so aptly put it, 'Luther was a great deal more compelling than gravity.' Throughout the rest of his life Bach would never turn from his Lutheran heritage, and he would never give up his citizenship in the town so steeped in Lutheran memorabilia. He often attached his place of origin to his signature: 'Johann Sebastian Bach *Isenacus*' or '*ISBI*'.

Bach's religious roots were deeply embedded in the soil of the Lutheran Reformation; his musical roots were deeply embedded in the same soil. Most

*Bach's religious roots were
deeply embedded in the soil
of the Lutheran Reformation;
his musical roots were deeply
embedded in the same soil.*

directly his roots, both religious and musical, were his family roots. When he was fifty years old, he compiled a genealogy of the numerous musicians in his family and called it the 'Origin of the Musical Bach Family' (hereafter Genealogy). The origin was his great-great-grandfather Veit Bach, who died in 1619. In a note in the Genealogy, Bach wrote that Veit was a baker in Hungary. Forced to flee from that country because of his Lutheran faith, he settled in the small Thuringian town of Wechmar, where he found religious security and continued his baker's trade. While waiting for the flour to be ground, he enjoyed playing his little guitar to the rhythmic accompaniment of the mill wheels. With a mixture of amusement and pride, Bach noted that this was the source of music in his family.

From that humble beginning sprang several generations of musicians who spread out from Wechmar to occupy musical positions in towns and churches throughout Thuringia. Bach's Obituary, written by his son Carl Philipp Emanuel and pupil Johann Friedrich Agricola, notes that although this family had 'received a love and aptitude for music as a gift of Nature', its members did not have ambitions that reached beyond Thuringia. They were 'well satisfied with their native land and with their station in life', preferring 'the approval of the rulers in whose domain they were born, and the approval of a throng of their faithful countrymen' to the praise of foreigners.

In addition to their strong sense of loyalty to place, religion, and each other, the Bach family was a cheerful, convivial lot. Bach's earliest biographer, Johann Nikolaus Forkel (1749–1818), painted this portrait of their family reunions:

Portrait of Johann Ambrosius Bach (1645–1695), father of Johann Sebastian.

As the company wholly consisted of cantors, organists, and town musicians, who had all to do with the Church, and as it was besides a general custom at the time to begin everything with Religion, the first thing they did when they were assembled, was to sing a chorale. From this pious commencement they proceeded to drolleries which often made a very great contrast with it. For now they sang popular songs, the contents of which were partly comic and partly naughty, all together and extempore, but in such a manner that the several parts thus extemporized made a kind of harmony together, the words, however, in every part being different. They called this kind of extemporary harmony a Quodlibet, and not only laughed heartily at it themselves, but excited an equally hearty and irresistible laughter in everybody that heard them.

The first of Veit's descendants to settle in Eisenach was Johann Christoph, a son of Sebastian's great uncle Heinrich. (There are ten Johann Christophs in the Genealogy! One of the others was Bach's uncle, the twin brother of his father; another was Bach's oldest brother.) This Johann Christoph, a cousin once removed, moved from Arnstadt to Eisenach in 1665 to take up the post of organist at St George's Church. He was an excellent composer, the best of the Bach clan before Johann Sebastian. In the Genealogy Bach called him 'profound'. Another indication of Bach's admiration for the music of

Bach's family tree is depicted in this diagram.

Engraving of the town
of Eisenach, where Bach
was born.

Engraving of the town of Eisenach, where Bach was born.

this older relative, as well as for some of his other ancestors, is a manuscript collection of scores called the *Altbachisches Archiv* (Old-Bach Archive), of which he was the proud custodian late in his life. Johann Christoph is the composer most frequently represented in the Old-Bach Archive, and Bach is known to have performed some of his pieces in the churches in Leipzig. Among them was the cantata 'Es erhub sich ein Streit im Himmel' ('And there was war in heaven'), an impressive setting of Revelation 12:7–12 for two five-part choirs and an orchestra of strings, bassoon, four trumpets, tympani, and continuo.

Sebastian's parents, Johann Ambrosius and Maria Elisabetha (*née* Lämmerhirt), were the next Bachs to settle in Eisenach. They moved from

Erfurt, their home town, to Eisenach in 1671. They had married in 1668, and brought their second son, the four-month-old Johann Christoph, with them to Eisenach. Their first born son had died before he was six months old. Six more children were born to them in Eisenach, the last being Johann Sebastian.

Like so many other Bachs, Ambrosius was a musician. In Erfurt he had been employed as a violinist, a member of the *Stadtpfeifer* (literally, town pipers). He moved to Eisenach when he procured the position of *Hausmann*, director of the *Stadtpfeifer*. He was highly respected for his virtuous Christian character as well as for his musicianship. A report from the Eisenach town chronicle praised his 1672 Easter music lavishly. No music like it had ever been heard in Eisenach, not even when Duke Wilhelm visited or when Duke Johann Georg was installed.

Despite his success in Eisenach, Ambrosius was ready to accept a position as a *Stadtpfeifer* back in Erfurt in 1684, but the duke and the town council refused to dismiss him. So Sebastian, most fittingly, was born in Eisenach with its rich associations with Luther and its strong musical heritage.

The Bach household was crowded and busy. It housed not only the parents and children, but also apprentices and journeymen who worked for Ambrosius. In addition, other relatives were sometimes taken in. Much of the busyness was related to music – teaching, practising, copying scores and parts, repairing instruments, and the like – which Sebastian could observe and eventually participate in. When he got to be old enough he could also observe and perhaps help his father with his work in the town and church. Ambrosius and his *Stadtpfeifer* were required to perform at the town hall at 10:00 a.m. and 5:00 p.m. daily. They also performed at church services, weddings, funerals, and civic events. When Ambrosius additionally became a member of a musical ensemble at the ducal court, Sebastian had occasion to hear and observe music-making in the court as well. Chorales and 'tower music' in the town square; chorales, organ music, cantatas, and motets in church; and suites and sonatas in the court – all these different types of music were gathered and stored in the memory of young Sebastian all the while his father was also teaching him violin and perhaps other instruments.

Cousin Johann Christoph provided opportunities for Sebastian to observe the life and work of another type of musician. Christoph was an organist, not a *Stadtpfeifer* like Ambrosius. Furthermore, unlike Ambrosius, Christoph was a composer. So he was a model and inspiration in two areas that would be so important in Sebastian's later life. Here in his own town and family was a skilled organist and harpsichordist who was also an excellent composer.

Further musical influences and training began when seven-year-old Sebastian enrolled in St George's Latin School. Like Luther before him, he sang in the school's *Chorus musicus*, a choir that provided polyphonic music for church services and special secular occasions. Its repertory stretched back as far as the early sixteenth century to composers like Ludwig Senfl and Josquin Desprez (favourite composers of Luther), through early seventeenth-century composers like Michael Praetorius and Heinrich Schütz (the greatest Lutheran composer before Bach) to contemporary composers like his cousin Johann Christoph – certainly a rich heritage and a solid foundation for a young musician!

We have no evidence of Sebastian being enrolled in school before his name appears on the rolls of St George's Latin School. But since it was the law in Eisenach that all children from age five to twelve must attend school,

he probably attended somewhere else before he enrolled in the Latin school, most likely a German school in nearby Fleischgasse. Religious instruction had primacy in the curricula in all schools in Lutheran territories. The Bible, Luther's Small Catechism, and the hymnal supplied the foundation for education.

St George's School had a reputation for excellence and attracted students from a wide area. Sebastian was a very good student. He progressed rapidly through the grades. He entered *quinta* (fifth level) in 1692 at the age of seven. (Unlike our numbering, the numbers in that system descended as the student advanced – *quinta, quarta, tertia*, etc.) Sebastian was younger than any of his brothers were when they entered, an indication that he entered at an unusually young age. After two years, the normal amount of time to complete a grade, he had risen to fourteenth in a class that began with ninety students. He then moved up to *quarta*, and after only one year graduated twenty-third of sixty-four.

Sebastian's family, church, school, and Eisenach itself provided a rich religious, educational, and musical environment in which to grow. But his years in Eisenach with his immediate family would be few. Tragedy struck before he turned ten years old, tragedy that forced him from his home town and paternal home.

Chapter 2

ORPHAN, STUDENT, AND BROADENING MUSICAL HORIZONS: OHRDRUF AND LÜNEBURG (1695–1703)

Death was a frequent visitor to the Bach family. Death, of course, comes to all. But when families are larger, when infant mortality rates are higher, and when other early deaths are more frequent, the likelihood increases that those who live a normal lifespan will experience an inordinate number of deaths of close family members. So it was with Bach. He outlived his parents and all his siblings; he also saw eleven of his twenty children to their graves.

Deaths of close family members began early for Sebastian. By the time he had lived barely six years, four of his siblings had died. A six-month-old brother died several years before Sebastian was born, and a ten-year-old brother and six-year-old sister died within his first fourteen months. Of course, Sebastian did not literally experience the first of those deaths, and he would have had no memory of the second, and little, if any, of the third. But he would have heard about those three siblings as they were remembered by other family members. He would have had many of his own memories of the fourth sibling, Johann Balthasar, who was living at home when he died, working as an apprentice *Stadtpfeifer* to his father. He was eighteen; Sebastian was six.

After Balthasar's death Sebastian experienced the deaths of two more relatives within a short time. A year after Balthasar's death a cousin died. This cousin, like Balthasar, was an apprentice to Ambrosius. He was one of two siblings who lived in the Bach household after their parents died during a plague. By the spring of 1694, when Sebastian entered *quarta* at St George's School, yet another close relative had died – his uncle Johann Christoph, twin brother of his father. Johann Christoph was a town and court musician in nearby Arnstadt, about 35 miles from Eisenach. Bach's son Carl Philipp Emanuel described the extraordinary closeness between the twins, a closeness that makes it likely that the two families were also close. 'They loved each other extremely,' Carl said. Their speech, manner of thinking, and music-making were the same, and they looked so much alike that even 'their wives could not tell them apart'. And he added, 'If one fell ill the other did, too. In short, the one [Ambrosius] died soon after the other.'

But before Ambrosius died, his wife, Maria Elisabetha, died. All we know about her death is this terse announcement: '3 May 1694. Buried, Johann Ambrosius Baach's wife – without fee.' Soon after his wife's death Ambrosius became seriously ill. He died in February 1695, a year and a half after his twin brother and less than a year after his wife. Sebastian, not quite ten years old, was now an orphan.

It is tempting to speculate about the effect these deaths had on Sebastian. Did he feel abandoned? Was he angry? Did he suppress his grief by working especially hard at school, or by intensifying his music practice? Did he find comfort in music, or in his larger family? No doubt the presence of a large extended family helped. Beyond that we can only guess. But we do not have to guess what he was taught about death. In school he would have learned articles of faith such as the following from Luther's Small Catechism:

I believe that Jesus Christ ... is my Lord, who has redeemed me ... from sin, death, and the power of the devil ... with his holy, precious blood and his innocent suffering and death, so that I may be his own and live under him in his kingdom ... just as he is risen from the dead and lives and rules eternally.

I believe that ... on the last day he will raise me and all the dead and give eternal life to me together with all believers in Christ.

Since the Bible and the hymnal were as much a part of the curriculum as the catechism, the beliefs articulated in the catechism would have been reinforced by Bible verses and chorales – and not only in school. Outside of school Sebastian would have heard Bible verses in church and perhaps recited them at home. He would have sung chorales frequently in church and at home, and even heard them played by the *Stadtpfeifer* in the town square.

What would he have recited, sung, and heard repeatedly? He would certainly have learned Paul's words from Romans 6:4, because they are quoted in the Small Catechism:

Thus we indeed are buried with him through baptism into death, so that, as Christ was raised from the dead by the glory of the Father, we too might walk in newness of life.

And since the memorization of Psalms was an important part of the curriculum, he would have known many comforting verses like Psalm 23:4 and 6:

Even though I already wander in the dark valley, I fear no misfortune, for you are with me; your rod and staff comfort me ... Goodness and mercy shall follow me all my life, and I shall dwell in the house of the Lord for ever.

Sebastian would have known Luther's great Easter chorale, 'Christ lag in Todes Banden' ('Christ lay in the bonds of death'), with its imagery of Christ's death swallowing death, and he would also have known some of the many comforting hymns that arose out of the terrible times of the

There can be little doubt that however child-like his understanding at the time, such beliefs, which the mature Bach would later express in his music with great depth and conviction, were already comforting to young Sebastian.

Thirty Years War. Further, there are comforting texts aplenty in the Old-Bach Archive. He might have heard Johann Michael Bach's simple but movingly beautiful motet that combines words of Job 19:25 – 'I know that my Redeemer lives, and afterward he will raise me from the earth' – with the first verse of the chorale 'Christus der ist mein Leben':

> *Christ is my life,*
> *to die is my reward,*
> *to Jesus I yield myself,*
> *with joy I now depart.*

Or, for another example, 'Unser Leben ist ein Schatten' ('Our life is but a shadow'), a motet attributed to his great-uncle Johann, combines depressing words about the brevity and futility of life from Job with the comforting words of Jesus recorded in John 11:25: 'I am the resurrection and the life. Whoever believes in me, he shall live, though he dies, and whoever lives and believes in me shall never die.' We do not know if Sebastian heard these particular pieces as a boy, but they are representative of much that he must have heard.

We might wonder how deeply a ten-year-old would understand such articles of faith, but there can be little doubt that however childlike his understanding at the time, such beliefs, which the mature Bach would later express in his music with great depth and conviction, were already comforting to young Sebastian.

Ambrosius remarried a few months after his wife's death. His new wife, Barbara Margaretha (*née* Keul), had been widowed twice before. Her first husband died just four months after the wedding. He was a cousin of Ambrosius who, according to the Genealogy, was 'a good musician and a skilful builder of various newly invented instruments'. Her second husband, a deacon at Arnstadt, died after four-and-a-half years of marriage. So when Ambrosius died just three months after their wedding, Barbara Margaretha became a widow for a third time. She was only thirty-seven and was left with the responsibility to care for five children – her own two daughters plus the three youngest living children of Ambrosius and Maria Elisabetha. This was too much to expect of her. So she returned to Arnstadt with her two daughters, and other arrangements were made for Sebastian and his siblings. The eighteen-year-old sister, Marie Salome, went to live in Erfurt with relatives; the two boys, ten-year-old Sebastian and thirteen-year-old Johann Jacob, went to Ohrdruf to live with their older brother Johann Christoph and his wife. They were expecting their first child when their younger brothers moved in.

Ohrdruf was a small town, the capital of the small county of Gleichen. It is located at the edge of the Thuringian Forest about 25 miles southeast of Eisenach. Of particular importance for Sebastian were its church, St Michael's, and its school, the *Lyceum Illustre Gleichense*.

The Lyceum was founded in the sixteenth century by the duke of Gleichen. It enjoyed considerable renown and attracted students from other parts of Germany. Its curriculum and methods were influenced by the ideas of Jan Amos Comenius (1592–1670), the great Moravian educational reformer. As at St George's School in Eisenach, the curriculum at the Lyceum was heavily theological, but it also included music (which Luther called the 'handmaid of theology'), arithmetic, Latin, beginning Greek, and ancient history. As a

*As a student at the Lyceum,
Sebastian continued to make
exceptional progress.*

student at the Lyceum, Sebastian continued to make exceptional progress. It is not clear exactly when or at what level he entered the Lyceum, but by July 1696 he had finished *tertia* ranked fourth in his class. The following July, at twelve the youngest in his class, he graduated to *secunda* ranked first. In July 1699, at fourteen, when he graduated to *prima*, he ranked second even though he was four years younger than the normal age.

In moving from his parental home in Eisenach to his brother's home in Ohrdruf, Sebastian moved from the musical environment of a *Hausmann* with a focus on wind and string instruments to that of a church musician with a focus on organ. Christoph's house was near St Michael's Church, where he served as organist. He was a fine organist who had studied in Erfurt with Johann Pachelbel. Christoph was Sebastian's first keyboard teacher. He laid the foundation for his younger brother's unparalleled mastery in organ performance and composition.

Christoph is usually perceived as the villain in an oft-told story. Apparently Sebastian very quickly learned the music Christoph gave him to practise. But Christoph also owned a manuscript that was off-limits to Sebastian. It contained pieces by some of the best composers of the previous and current generations, including Pachelbel, Christoph's revered teacher. Sebastian yearned to learn that music, but Christoph denied him access to the manuscript. So at night, when all were asleep, Sebastian went to the cabinet in which the manuscript was kept, put his little hand through the grillwork in the locked door, rolled up the manuscript, and pulled it out. He copied the music by moonlight, and after six months had all the music in a manuscript of his own. But when Christoph discovered it, he took it away. The Obituary describes Sebastian's sorrow as being like that of 'a miser whose ship, sailing for Peru, has foundered with its cargo of a hundred thousand thalers'.

There is no way of knowing Christoph's motive for depriving Sebastian of his precious, hard-earned manuscript. It could just as likely have been well-meaning, having to do with pedagogical method, as something malignant like jealousy. There are no clues regarding his motives in the story. What it does reveal is that Sebastian was already showing a characteristic that would remain with him throughout his life: an insatiable appetite to learn music coupled with a dogged determination to satisfy it, whatever the cost in hard work.

We do not know when Sebastian began composing, but three short chorale fughettas, BWV 749, 750, and 756, are obviously student compositions. Their authorship is in doubt, but they may represent the type of exercises that brother Christoph could have given him when he was barely, or not yet, a teenager.

After one year brother Jacob returned to Eisenach to be apprenticed to his father's successor. He was fourteen at the time, and Christoph and his wife were expecting their second child. Sebastian stayed on for another four years, but by then Christoph's house and income may have been too small to support his growing family and Sebastian. So on 15 March 1700, a few days before his fifteenth birthday, Sebastian left Ohrdruf for Lüneburg.

Lüneburg was about 200 miles from Ohrdruf and about four times as large. None of Sebastian's relatives had moved that far from their Thuringian homes and none had an academic education beyond what Sebastian had already achieved by the time he left Ohrdruf. If he had followed the normal course taken by his family members, he would have apprenticed

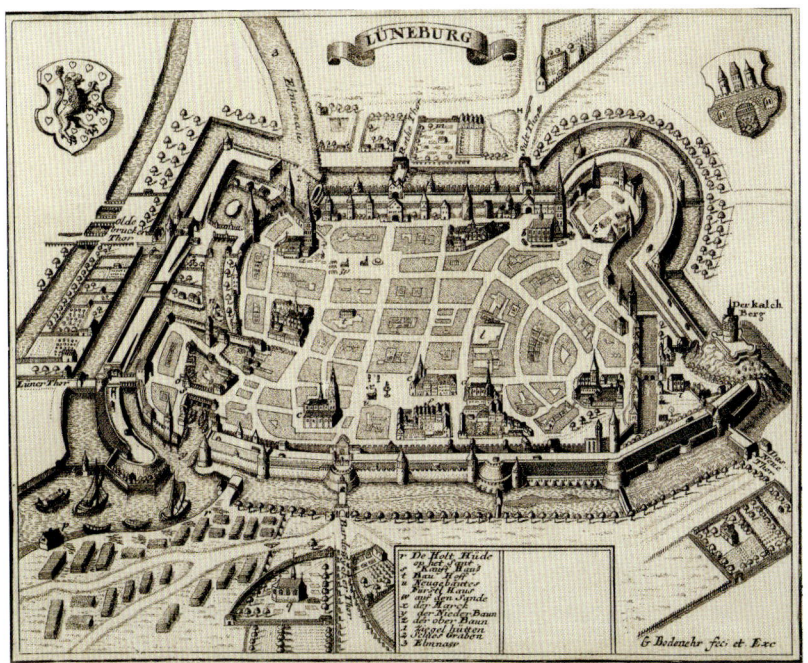

as a *Stadtpfeifer* or church organist. He was at the stage in life when they typically discontinued their academic education, were apprenticed for a few years, and then were ready to take up a musical position in town or church. Brother Johann Christoph had followed that path. Until the age of fifteen he had gone to school in Eisenach, where, as he wrote in an autobiographical note, he was 'educated in the Christian belief'. After that, because his father saw that he 'was more inclined towards music than towards the studies', he was apprenticed to Pachelbel for three years before taking a position as church organist.

It is logical to think that Christoph would have expected Sebastian to follow the same path. On the other hand he must have recognized that his younger brother, though enormously gifted in music, was not, like himself, disinclined 'towards the studies'. Whatever Christoph expected, an opportunity presented itself to Sebastian at a favourable moment, and he took advantage of that opportunity with or without his brother's blessing.

The opportunity was to enrol as a choral scholar at St Michael's School in Lüneburg. The school offered scholarships that paid tuition plus room and board for needy children with good voices. Sebastian

St Michael's Church in Lüneburg.

qualified on both counts: as an orphan he was needy, and the Obituary tells us that he had an 'uncommonly fine soprano voice'. The cantor in Ohrdruf, Elias Herda, had attended St Michael's, and it was most likely his recommendation that secured a place there for Sebastian and his schoolmate Georg Erdmann. Carrying a few belongings and travelling on foot, fifteen-year-old Sebastian and eighteen-year-old Georg arrived in Lüneburg by the end of March.

Sebastian finished his schooling at St Michael's, graduating from *prima* (the final level before university) in the spring of 1702. St Michael's had a high reputation for its strong liberal arts curriculum in the old Latin school tradition similar to that in the schools in Eisenach and Ohrdruf. So when he graduated he had a good, well-rounded education in Latin, classical literature and history, geography, arithmetic, and physics, with theology as the foundation. He was now prepared for university. Had he been so minded he could have gone on to study for a profession such as theology, medicine, or, like his friend Erdmann, law. But of course he never intended to enter any career other than music. Venturing to Lüneburg, beyond the geographical and educational boundaries of his family, was never intended to be a break from the family vocation.

For Sebastian the attractions of Lüneburg must have been at least as much musical as academic. The school had two choirs, the *chorus symphoniacus* and the smaller, more select *Mettenchor* (Matins Choir). Their repertories were drawn from a very large and rich music library. Among the composers represented were the late Renaissance master Orlando di Lasso, early seventeenth-century Italian masters like Claudio Monteverdi and Giacomo Carissimi, along with their German counterparts like Heinrich

Schütz and Johann Hermann Schein (one of Bach's predecessors at Leipzig), and later seventeenth-century Germans like Diedrich Buxtehude and Sebastian's cousin Johann Christoph and great-uncle Heinrich. While in Lüneburg Sebastian's exposure to organ music was as rich as his exposure to choral music. The organist at St John's Church was Georg Böhm, one of the outstanding north German organists of the time. He was also a fine composer. We do not know if Sebastian studied formally with Böhm, but he certainly heard Böhm's music and studied it carefully.

Sebastian's organ experiences were not limited to Böhm. Hamburg, Germany's largest city, was rich in musical culture. Since it was only about 35 miles from Lüneburg, Sebastian was able to make several trips there. He probably visited the Hamburg Opera directed by Reinhard Keiser. But Hamburg's greatest attractions for him were its organs and organists, in particular the great organ at St Catharine's Church and its organist, Johann Adam Reincken. Reincken's pedigree went back through his teacher Heinrich Scheidemann to the great Dutch composer and organist Jan Pieterszoon Sweelinck, 'father' of the north German school of organ playing and composition.

Sebastian's trips to Hamburg were musically profitable but taxing on his pocketbook. Later in his life he told the music theorist Friedrich Wilhelm Marpurg about an amusing experience he had during one of his trips. On his way back from Hamburg he found himself hungry, almost broke, and only about halfway home. While standing outside an inn contemplating his predicament, a window opened, and someone threw a couple of herring heads onto the garbage pile. He rushed to recover them and found, much to his surprise, a Danish ducat in each head! This gift from an unknown benefactor not only was sufficient to pay for a meal; it financed another trip to hear Reincken.

Sebastian also encountered French music while in Lüneburg. Celle, the seat of the dukes of Braunschwig-Lüneburg, was about 55 miles southwest of Lüneburg. Due to the influence of the duchess, a French Huguenot, the orchestra at Celle was made up of French players. We do not know whether Sebastian ever travelled to Celle to hear them play, but he had opportunities to hear them play in Lüneburg at the duchess's dower house.

Although Sebastian was in Lüneburg for only two years, it was a time when his alert ear gathered a wide range of musical influences beyond what Eisenach and Ohrdruf had provided. An expanded choral repertory, north German organ music, French dance music, and Italian operatic styles provided more musical seeds that would grow in his fertile mind. So when he finished *prima* at St Michael's School, he had completed a strong liberal arts education based on Lutheran theology, and his musical horizons had broadened extensively. We do not know when Sebastian left Lüneburg, but we do know that he applied for the position of organist at St James's Church in Sangerhausen. Despite his youth and inexperience he was offered the job, but the duke overruled the committee and appointed his own candidate to the position. Soon thereafter Sebastian obtained a position at the court of the duke of Weimar, but that brief part of his life is almost totally blank. All that remains is a record of two payments 'To the Lackey Baach'.

Chapter 3
CHURCH ORGANIST: ARNSTADT (1703–1707)

Bach's short-lived employment at Weimar had brought him back close to home – within about 50 miles of Eisenach. For the rest of his life he would rarely venture as far away as Lüneburg, and then only on brief excursions, not to live and work. After the duke had overruled his appointment at Sangerhausen, he found employment even closer to home. He was appointed organist at the New Church in Arnstadt, the oldest city in Thuringia. Its documented history goes back to the eighth century. Located at the edge of the Thuringian Forest about 35 miles from Eisenach, it had a population of about 4,000 in Bach's time. It was the capital of the region of Thuringia governed by the counts of Schwarzburg. Their castle, Schloss Neidick, was located in the centre of town.

There were three churches in Arnstadt. The largest and oldest was Our Lady's Church, built in the late thirteenth century. Almost as old was the Upper Church, formerly the Barefoot Friars' (Franciscan) Church. This was the church attended by the count's retinue and many of Arnstadt's leading citizens. The third church was originally St Boniface's Church. Its building was destroyed by fire in 1581. Lack of funds prevented rebuilding the church for nearly a century, but by the 1670s overcrowding in the other churches made a new building necessary. Countess Sophia provided funds for the rebuilding that took place between 1676 and 1683. St Boniface's Church then became known as the New Church. A new organ was commissioned from Johann Friedrich Wender, one of the leading organ-builders in Germany. The contract stipulated completion in 1699, but the work was not completed until 1703. In the meantime Andreas Börner, son-in-law of court organist Christoph Herthun, was appointed organist even though the incomplete instrument could only be used for accompaniment

The city of Arnstadt, where Bach was appointed organist.

purposes. When it was finished, the New Church had a relatively small but excellent organ.

Bach had deep family roots in Arnstadt. His father, Ambrosius, and his uncle Johann Christoph had worked there. Other Bachs had preceded them. Great-uncle Heinrich served Arnstadt's two main churches as organist for more than fifty years, and Caspar, a son of Veit, was employed there as a carpet-maker from as early as about 1620. His three sons were employed as musicians in the service of the count of Schwarzburg-Arnstadt.

Bach had other Arnstadt connections as well. Christoph Herthun, Heinrich Bach's successor, married one of Heinrich's daughters, and two sisters-in-law of Martin Feldhaus, a leading citizen, were married to two of Bach's cousins – one to Johann Christoph of Eisenach, the other to Christoph's brother Johann Michael, who would later become Bach's father-in-law.

Bach's appointment seems to have been pre-arranged and not without the help of his connections. In July 1703 he was invited to inspect and exhibit the newly completed organ. Why was he invited instead of Börner, the experienced incumbent? What credentials did this inexperienced eighteen-year-old have? In playing he had been instructed by his brother Christoph between the ages of ten and fifteen years, and the following two years gave him the opportunity to hear great organists in Lüneburg and Hamburg. But he never had sustained tutelage under a leading organist, as Christoph had under Pachelbel. His situation was similar with respect to knowledge of the mechanical workings of the instrument, except that in this he had no formal training at all. But from as early as his time in Ohrdruf, if not already in Eisenach, he had many opportunities to observe the mechanics of various organs and to see the craftsmen at work tuning and maintaining them.

Nevertheless, despite his inexperience, he must have been qualified to test and exhibit the new organ, and even to take up the position as the New Church organist. There can be little doubt that he was a better organist than Börner; indeed he was probably better than most organists in Thuringia. Were he not, it is unlikely that even his family connections would have been sufficient to get him invited to inaugurate the fine new instrument in the New Church, let alone be appointed as its organist. But family connections certainly helped, as did the influence of Martin Feldhaus and Count Anton Günther, who had high regard for the Bach family.

The certificate of appointment required Bach to show himself 'industrious and reliable in the office, vocation, and practice of the art and science' entrusted to him. He was 'to appear promptly on Sundays, feast days, and other days of public divine service'. In a normal week, that would be four services. He was also to see to the maintenance of the instrument. In his daily life he was expected to fear God, be sober and peaceful, shun bad company, and in general to act appropriately before God and all in authority.

Bach received a good salary, almost twice what Börner had received. Half of the money came from the church treasury; the other half came from the beer tax. In addition he received money for room and board, money that came from the Hospital of St George and St James, an institution that provided residence and care for old people. Although Bach's duties as the New Church organist included some playing for services at the hospital, it is a bit suspicious that Feldhaus was both the inspector of hospitals and the owner of the house in which Bach lived. This arrangement, though seemingly self-serving on Feldhaus's part, was advantageous for Bach – and it would prove to have an unexpected advantage. Feldhaus was godfather of Maria Barbara Bach.

CHURCH ORGANIST: ARNSTADT (1703–1707)

She came to live with him after the death of her mother in 1704 had left her without a living parent. A few years later she would become Bach's wife.

Arnstadt offered Bach opportunities for informal continuing education in theology and church music. His superior in Arnstadt was the Reverend Johann Gottfried Olearius, superintendent of the Arnstadt churches and a member of a family of Lutheran theologians. Bach heard sermons week after week from preachers supervised by Olearius, and he would have engaged with Olearius and the other pastors in theological discussions at least insofar as they pertained to the worship services. Olearius was also a musician. He had served as music director at Our Lady's Church in Halle, and he knew the Bach family. Bach's great-uncle Heinrich had served under Olearius as organist in Arnstadt, and Olearius had preached the sermon at his funeral. Olearius had a son, Johann Christoph, who was the librarian and a deacon at the New Church. He was also a hymnologist, and during the time Bach was in Arnstadt he was writing a commentary on the hymns of the Church. Bach must have benefited greatly from conversations about theology and music with both father and son. Later he would learn from yet another Olearius. Johann, the younger brother of Johann Gottfried, was the author of a five-volume set of Bible commentaries listed in the inventory of Bach's personal library.

Bach's workload at the New Church was relatively light, leaving him ample time to practise and compose. As the Obituary put it, 'Here he really showed the first fruits of his application to the art of organ playing and to composition, which he had learned chiefly by the observation of the works of the most famous and proficient composers of his day, and by the fruits of his

This coloured engraving by
Matthäus Merian depicts
Lübeck's cityscape.

own reflection upon them.' We have already noted several of those 'famous
and proficient composers'. The Obituary provides additional names, most
importantly Diedrich Buxtehude, organist at St Mary's Church in Lübeck.
Among north German organists, Buxtehude was held in highest regard, not
only for his organ-playing, but for his compositions as well. In addition to
many impressive organ works, he composed sacred vocal music in German
and Latin, suites and variations for harpsichord, and chamber music, an
output that approaches the breadth that would later characterize Bach's.

Buxtehude's work had attracted Georg Frideric Handel to Lübeck in
1703; it attracted Bach in 1705. In mid-October Bach set out on foot for
Lübeck, some 250 miles away, to hear and learn from Buxtehude, who was
nearing seventy years of age and looking for a successor. Was Bach looking
not only to learn from Buxtehude but also to succeed him? If so, did he
know that there was a stipulation that Buxtehude's successor had to marry
his daughter, ten years Bach's senior and apparently not very attractive? It
was a fairly common stipulation; Buxtehude had married his predecessor's
daughter, and his eventual successor would marry his daughter. Both
Handel and his friend Johann Mattheson lost interest in the position because
of that stipulation. Whether Bach knew of it or not, he returned to Arnstadt
with neither a job offer nor a marriage engagement. What he did return
with was greater comprehension of 'one and another aspect of his art', as
he reported to the Arnstadt consistory. Indeed, his stay in Lübeck was, as
the Obituary laconically put it, 'not without profit'. But it was also one of
several incidents that put a strain on the relationship between Bach and his
employers. He had left Arnstadt in mid-October 1705, having been granted
a leave of four weeks, but he did not return until mid-February – a period

of four months that included the entire Advent, Christmas and Epiphany seasons!

Although his extended absence was irresponsible, it is understandable. He had little systematic tutelage in composition; he learned composition mainly through listening, improvising, and studying scores (many of which he had to copy himself). From his earliest days he absorbed the music that surrounded him in his musically rich environments, and his inquisitive nature led him to look even beyond them to seek out whatever music was within his reach, near at hand or far. Recall, for example, Sebastian copying the forbidden manuscript by moonlight and his trips to Hamburg. It is no wonder that he found it difficult to limit his opportunity to hear Buxtehude's music, music that would provide a powerful stimulus for his own composition.

We do not know how much composing Bach did at Arnstadt, but we do know that the surviving works that can be assigned with reasonable certainty to his Arnstadt years (or a little before) are all keyboard works. Two capriccios for harpsichord were probably composed in Arnstadt. He wrote one in honour of his brother Johann Christoph (BWV 993), whose teaching he must have appreciated despite being deprived of the precious manuscript he had copied so diligently. The other is the well-known *Capriccio sopra la lontananza de il fratello dilettissimo* ('Capriccio on the Departure of the Most Dear Brother'), BWV 992. The departing brother is usually thought to be Johann Jacob who joined the Swedish army while Bach was in Arnstadt. There is certainly something attractive about Bach composing a capriccio for each of his two surviving brothers, but in lieu of specific dates for the piece and for Jacob's departure we cannot positively link the piece with the event. Furthermore *il fratello* does not necessarily refer to a sibling. It could be used to refer to a professional

*Whatever Bach's early
achievements as an organist and
composer, the Arnstadt consistory
was not entirely satisfied with their
young employee.*

colleague or a friend. Whoever *il fratello* was, young Bach must have had a good time writing this clever, if rather naïve, piece. It is a programmatic work whose six movements depict stages of parting. Friends try to dissuade the departing brother from leaving, first by coaxing, then by frightening him with descriptions of the dangers he might encounter. These attempts to dissuade are followed by lamentation, leave-taking, the song of the postilion, and a fugue based on the post-horn fanfare.

Bach's toccatas for harpsichord, BWV 912–915, are also thought to date from the Arnstadt years as are his earliest preludes and fugues for organ. Both the harpsichord and organ works are characterized by the kind of youthful flamboyance found in the well-known Toccata in D Minor for organ, BWV 565.

The discovery in 1984 of thirty-one chorale preludes, BWV 1090–1120, added considerably to our knowledge of Bach's compositional activity during his time in Arnstadt and before. Some of them are modelled after the works of his older cousins, Johann Christoph and Johann Michael, and of Pachelbel. Others show the influence of north German organists Böhm and Buxtehude. Böhm's influence is also clear in Bach's chorale partitas, BWV 766–768, although, in its surviving form, BWV 768 seems to be a later revision, an example of Bach's penchant for improving his own earlier works.

Whatever Bach's early achievements as an organist and composer, the Arnstadt consistory was not entirely satisfied with their young employee. In addition to his overstayed leave in Lübeck, consistory meeting minutes record complaints about Bach's organ-playing. When reprimanded for playing too long, he immediately went to the other extreme and played too short. He also made 'curious variations' in the chorales and put in 'many

Bernd Göbel's provocative statue of Bach as a young man, erected in Market Square, Arnstadt, in 1985.

strange tones', thereby confusing the congregation. One of Bach's chorale preludes that almost certainly originated in Arnstadt is 'Wie schön leuchtet der Morgenstern' ('How brightly shines the Morning Star'), BWV 739. It is a typically extravagant youthful work in which the chorale melody is developed and decorated in a rich variety of ways that perhaps sounded like 'curious variations' to the congregation. Some other early chorale settings, BWV 715, 722, 726, and 732 – sometimes referred to as 'Arnstadt chorales' – consist of elaborate chordal harmonizations of the chorale melody with elaborate improvisation-like flourishes between the phrases. Whether they date from Arnstadt or somewhat later, the flourishes and the highly chromatic harmonizations have the earmarks of a talented young (not to say immature) organist seeking to impress. They could very well exemplify the 'many strange tones' that confused the congregation.

Consistory minutes also report some of Bach's troubles with students, many of whom were barely (if at all) younger than he. The minutes of meetings in August 1705 record one of the best-known incidents in Bach's life: his fight in the market place with a senior student named Geyersbach. One evening Bach and his cousin Barbara Catharina were walking home from the Schloss Neidick when they happened upon a group of students in the marketplace. Geyersbach went after Bach 'with a stick' and demanded to know why Bach had made abusive remarks to him. Bach drew his sword, and in the ensuing brawl the two combatants had to be separated by the other students. In front of the consistory Bach accused Geyersbach of attacking him first and claimed that he reached for his sword only in order to defend himself. Geyersbach, in turn, claimed that Bach drew his sword first. Barbara Catharina's testimony corroborated Bach's story (but was she an unbiased witness?). The consistory, probably realizing they could not sift the truth out of the conflicting stories, simply reprimanded Bach for his abusive language. But they also noted that he had a reputation for not getting along with students.

Consistory minutes record yet another complaint: Bach had invited a *frembde Jungfer* to make music in the choir loft. Who was this 'unfamiliar maiden'? The favoured answer is that she was Maria Barbara, Bach's future wife. But she would hardly have been referred to as *frembde*, that is, 'unfamiliar' or 'strange' or 'foreign'. Her father, Johann Michael Bach, was born in Arnstadt and was court organist there for a few years. He had left Arnstadt before Maria Barbara was born, but she came to Arnstadt after her mother died to live with her godfather, Martin Feldhaus, a well-known citizen. However, as Peter Williams has suggested, if *frembde* was used in the sense of 'unauthorized', the maiden could have been Maria Barbara. So we do not know.

But what we do know is that Bach would not be long for Arnstadt. Arnstadt had provided him with a good situation for growth: a comfortable salary, a theologically learned supervisor who was also knowledgable about music, a relatively light workload, a fine new organ and ample time to practise, a fruitful visit to Lübeck to learn from Buxtehude, and the opportunity to continue his initial efforts in composition. Even if he had not already been looking for another position when he went to Lübeck, it is clear that a variety of irritations, and probably a growing feeling that the possibilities were too limited, would soon cause him to look beyond Arnstadt for another place to serve.

Chapter 4
CHURCH ORGANIST: MÜHLHAUSEN (1707–1708)

The Arnstadt consistory's reprimand of Bach for inviting an 'unfamiliar [or unauthorized] maiden' into the choir loft appeared in the minutes of 11 November 1706. Three weeks later, on 2 December, the organist of St Blasius' Church in Mühlhausen died. Bach must have seen this as an opportunity not only to leave the vexations of his Arnstadt position, but also to go to a place of greater opportunity. Mühlhausen is about 35 miles from Arnstadt. In Thuringia in Bach's time it was second in size to Erfurt. It had become Lutheran in 1557 and now had no fewer than thirteen churches. The most important were St Mary's Church and St Blasius' Church, both housed in Gothic structures dating back to the thirteenth century. St Blasius had a history of fine organists dating back to the late sixteenth century. They had served as municipal music directors in addition to their duties as church organists. The two most recent were Johann Rudolf Ahle and his son Johann Georg, both of whom were also noted composers. Their diverse output of music includes a good amount of sacred choral music.

Bach seems to have been the only applicant who auditioned for the position. One other applicant was Johann Gottfried Walther. He submitted two compositions but later withdrew his application before auditioning. Walther, a distant relative of Bach, subsequently received an appointment in Weimar. When Bach later moved to Weimar, the two became close friends.

Bach's audition took place on Easter Sunday 24 April 1707. It is tempting to think that in addition to playing the organ, he performed Cantata 4, 'Christ lag in Todes Banden' ('Christ lay in the bonds of death'), based on Luther's great Easter chorale. There is no definite evidence for this, but it is the only surviving cantata that fits chronologically.

Bach received the appointment – probably, as at Arnstadt, a foregone conclusion. One of the Mühlhausen town councillors was Johann Hermann Bellstedt, who had family connections in Arnstadt. His brother's wife was a sister-in-law of Martin Feldhaus and the aunt of Bach's soon-to-be wife, Maria Barbara. Bellstedt, who may have been the one who recommended Bach for the position, was entrusted by the town council with negotiating Bach's salary. Bach asked for, and got, the same basic salary he had at Arnstadt plus the same emoluments his predecessor received, which his contract specified as 54 bushels of grain, 2 cords of wood, and 360 bundles of sticks. He was also provided with a wagon to move his belongings.

Mühlhausen wanted Bach, and Bach saw Mühlhausen as an attractive alternative to Arnstadt. St Blasius' Church had a larger organ, and although the official job description was very similar to Arnstadt's, the scope of his activity would be broader because, like his predecessors, he would also serve as music director for the town. Further, it is likely that he saw in Mühlhausen a serious commitment to sacred choral music. He probably saw the activity of the Ahles as composers of sacred choral music and the requirement to submit a choral composition as part of the application as indications of such a commitment. He must have been aware that the organ was in need of work, but was he aware that, however rich Mühlhausen's musical tradition had been, especially in its prime under the elder Ahle, the musical situation was now somewhat in decline, and that whatever the commitment to sacred choral music was or had been, it would turn out to be not in line with his own ideals? But however he saw the situation, he must have seen Mühlhausen as having greater potential for fulfilling his ambitions than Arnstadt. In particular, he saw this position, as he would

The historical centre of
Mühlhausen, with St Peter's
Church in the foreground.

later say, as an opportunity to work towards the goal of 'a well-regulated church music'. He was ready to take up the challenge of that goal in this new environment.

Bach officially took up his new position on 1 July 1707. On 18 September his uncle Tobias Lämmerhirt died and left him 50 florins, a most welcome financial boost for Bach and Maria Barbara, who were to be married just one month later. The wedding took place in a small church in Dornheim, just a few miles from Arnstadt, where the pastor was a friend of the family. We can assume the wedding was a festive affair with many Bachs participating in the music-making. It is possible that Cantata 196 was performed at the wedding. Its small-scale scoring lends itself to performance in a small church, and its text, Psalm 115:12–15, is suitable for a wedding.

> *The Lord is mindful of us and blesses us.*
> *He blesses the house of Israel;*
> *he blesses the house of Aaron.*
> *He blesses those who fear the Lord,*
> *both small and great.*
> *May the Lord bless you more and more,*
> *you and your children.*
> *You are blessed by the Lord,*
> *who has made heaven and earth.*

More particularly, as Mary Dalton Greer points out, the text was especially suitable for Bach's wedding because contemporary editions of Luther's translation of the Bible often gave Psalm 115 the heading 'Gott allein die Ehre,' the German version of the Latin motto that Bach put at the end of many of his scores – 'Soli Deo Gloria' ('To God alone be glory'). Further, Bach identified his vocation with that of the Old Testament Temple musicians, the Levites of the House of Aaron. We do not know how consciously Bach was making that identification at this time, but naming his goal as a well-regulated church music points in that direction. Markings in his Calov Bible later in life (see Chapter 13) show that he came to make the identification very consciously.

The small village church in Dornheim where Bach and Maria Barbara were wed in 1707.

Maria Barbara, daughter of Johann Michael Bach, was Bach's cousin twice removed, legally distant enough for marriage. We know very little about her, but since she came from a musical family, we suspect she was at least somewhat musical. The Obituary says she was 'hale and hearty', and describes the marriage 'blissful'.

Beyond his weekly duties in the church services, a high priority for Bach when he began his work at Mühlhausen was the renovation and expansion of the organ at St Blasius' Church. He drew up plans for the work which the council approved in February 1708. The work was assigned to Wender, who had built Bach's organ in Arnstadt. When he requested dismissal from Mühlhausen, Bach said that he had fulfilled his duty 'in delivering the project for remedying the faults of the organ'. In addition he said that he had worked to improve the church music not only in Mühlhausen but also the church music that was 'growing up in almost every township'. To that end he had acquired, 'not without cost, a good store of the choicest church compositions'.

Bach's own surviving choral compositions from the time are few and seem to have been written mainly for special occasions, not regular church services. We have already mentioned the possibility that Cantata 4 was written as a test piece for his audition and that Cantata 196 was written for a wedding, perhaps his own. No occasion for Cantata 150 is known. It might even pre-date Bach's time in Mühlhausen. Cantata 131, 'Aus der Tiefen rufe ich, Herr, zu dir' ('Out of the depths I call, Lord, to you'), was written at the request of Pastor Georg Eilmar. We do not know the occasion, but its text, a cry for mercy which includes Psalm 130 in its entirety, suggests that it was for a special penitential service. An occasion for such a service could have been the fire of 30 May 1707, which destroyed hundreds of homes and other buildings in the St Blasius parish.

The fact that the request for Cantata 131 came from Pastor Eilmar, pastor of St Mary's Church, rather than from Bach's own pastor at St Blasius', is an indication of the friendship that had developed between the Bachs and the Eilmars. Later, after the Bachs had moved to Weimar, Eilmar became the godfather of their first child, Catharina Dorothea, and his daughter the godmother of their second child, Wilhelm Friedemann. That friendship may have resulted in part from conflict over music between the two pastors. Johann Adolf Frohne, pastor at St Blasius', was not in favour of figural church music (that is, elaborate music for voices and instrumental ensemble). Eilmar, on the other hand, favoured figural music and was apparently Bach's ally in trying to promote it in Mühlhausen.

Another occasion for which Bach had the opportunity to compose a cantata was the service that commemorated the town council change on 4 February 1708. As a free imperial city, Mühlhausen was ruled by the emperor. But under him, the city was ruled by a council of forty-eight citizens. The council was divided into three groups of sixteen, fourteen *Ratsherren* (councillors) and two *Bürgomeister* (mayors). The three groups rotated yearly so that each group was responsible for the management of the city for one year out of three. The yearly rotation was marked by an elaborate ceremony. An eighteenth-century account of one of these ceremonies says that it began between 7:00 and 8:00 a.m. with the ringing of the large bell. Then there was a procession from the city

*However excellent
Mühlhausen's musical
tradition had been, the city had
never heard music like this!*

hall to the church – in 1708 that was St Mary's, Eilmar's church. The
outgoing council led the procession followed by the incoming council.
Two ensembles 'with trumpets and drums' made music. The service at
the church began with the singing of chorales followed by a sermon. It
concluded with 'vocal and instrumental music wishing the new council
good fortune'.

For the service Bach wrote Cantata 71, *Gott ist mein König* ('God is my
King'). It is figural music to the hilt, perhaps as much to make a case for
his own and Eilmar's position on church music as it was to add splendour
to the ceremonial event. It is scored for choir, a solo quartet, and four
instrumental choirs: a brass choir of trumpets and drums; a flute choir of
recorders and cello; a reed choir of oboes and bassoon; and a string choir
of violins, viola, and violone. These must have sounded splendid coming
from the various galleries and lofts in St Mary's Church. However excellent
Mühlhausen's musical tradition had been, the city had never heard music
like this!

The cantata causes some puzzlement today because it was composed
for a 'secular' event, but it has a sacred text, mostly from the Bible. The
puzzlement betrays an anachronistic idea about the separation of Church
and State. There was no such separation in Lutheran Germany in Bach's
time. The opening chorus quotes Psalm 74:12, 'God is my King'. On
behalf of all the people, including the councillors, the choir professes
that all earthly authority is under God, from whom their help comes. In
the following movement, solo voices represent the 'old ones', that is, the
outgoing councillors. They pray for patience and protection from sin and
disgrace so that they may wear their 'grey hair with honour'. Then the

choir, again representing the people, sings Moses' benediction on the tribe of Asher and Abimelech's on Abraham:

> *May your old age be like your youth.*
> *And God is with you in all that you do.*
> (DEUTERONOMY 33:25 AND GENESIS 21:22).

Then they praise God for his universal rule:

> *Day and night are yours.*
> *You make both sun and stars to have their sure orbit.*
> *You fix the boundaries of every land.*
> (PSALM 74:16–17)

They petition him for protection:

> *Do not give the soul of your turtle-doves to the enemy.*
> (PSALM 74:19)

Finally, they ask for his blessing on the new government, for peace and prosperity, and for happiness, safety, and victory that will 'delight you, [Emperor] Joseph'.

The cantata must have been favourably accepted by the Mühlhausen authorities. They published not only the text of the cantata, as was customary, but also the performing parts. The following year, and perhaps the year after, they asked Bach to write another cantata for the council exchange even though he had already resigned and moved to Weimar. He obliged, but Cantata 71 is the only one that has survived. It also has the distinction of being the only one of all Bach's cantatas that was published during his lifetime.

However big an impression Cantata 71 made, it does not represent Bach's best work in Mühlhausen. That honour must go to Cantatas 4 and 106. Cantata 4 has eight movements, a sinfonia followed by movements for each of the seven verses of Luther's Easter chorale, 'Christ lag in Todes Banden' ('Christ lay in the bonds of death'). Each of the movements incorporates the chorale melody and uses the text verbatim. They are arranged symmetrically around the middle verse, which proclaims the central message of the resurrection: Christ's victory over death.

> *It was a strange and dreadful strife*
> *when life and death contended;*
> *the victory remained with life;*
> *the reign of death was ended.*
> *Stripped of power, no more it reigns,*
> *death's sting is lost forever!*
> *Alleluia!*
>
> (TR. RICHARD MASSIE)

Cantata 106, 'Gottes Zeit ist die allerbeste Zeit' ('God's time is the best time'), mixes Old and New Testament passages about God's law and his grace with chorale verses. After a beautifully serene opening sinfonia, the cantata moves from the inevitability of death to the promise Jesus made to

the criminal crucified next to him: 'Today you shall be with me in Paradise.' As a bass sings Jesus' words, an alto sings the words of another chorale by Luther, this one based the Song of Simeon (Luke 2:29–32):

> *In peace and joy I now depart*
> *According to God's will;*
> *For full of comfort is my heart*
> *So calm and still.*
> *So doth God his promise keep,*
> *And death to me is but a sleep.*
>
> (TR. CATHERINE WINKWORTH)

Cantata 106 was clearly written for a funeral, but we do not know for whom it was written. Nonetheless, in it Bach produced a Christian statement about death and salvation that is, as Alfred Dürr describes it, a 'work of genius such as even great masters seldom achieve. Here, in one stroke, the twenty-two-year-old composer left all his contemporaries far behind him.' Here, as in Cantata 4, Bach showed that he had learned his theology well, that he had reached an exceptional level of compositional skill, and that he was now well on his way to becoming unequalled in his ability to join the two.

Despite his youth, Bach was more than well equipped to broaden his service to the church to include composing cantatas on a regular basis. But Mühlhausen was not to be the place. In June 1708, after only eleven months in the job, Bach received an offer for another position. There is no indication that he had been actively looking. Had an offer not come up, he might have stayed in Mühlhausen for some time. An eventual move was inevitable, but an offer that was clearly a step up precipitated it earlier than expected. As Bach put it in his request for dismissal, 'Now, God has brought it to pass that an unexpected change should offer itself to me.'

His first reason for requesting dismissal was hindrance in working towards his goal.

Even though I should always have liked to work towards the goal, namely, a well-regulated church music, to the Glory of God and in conformance with your wishes … yet it has not been possible to accomplish all this without hindrance, and there are, at present, hardly any signs that in the future a change may take place (although it would rejoice the souls belonging to the church).

Bach did not specify what the hindrances were, but surely the major one was the pietist view that figural music was worldly ostentation. Only simple, easily accessible, 'heartfelt' music was acceptable. The literature on Bach typically describes the conflict in Mühlhausen as a clear-cut theological disagreement between the two pastors, the pietist Frohne and the orthodox Eilmar. No doubt opposition to figural church music in Mühlhausen was aided by Pastor Frohne's pietist-influenced view of music, but except in their extreme forms, pietism and orthodoxy were not oil and water. Orthodox theology was not at odds with the spiritual intensity and devout piety often taken to be exclusive characteristics of pietism. But at least with regard to music, orthodoxy and pietism did go in different directions. So however much there is of pietism in the texts of his cantatas, Bach could not accept pietism's musical limitations.

In addition to the musical reason for accepting the new offer, Bach openly admitted that there was a financial reason as well. On his current income, he said, 'however simple my manner of living, I can live but poorly, considering the house rent and other most necessary expenses'. (He could have added that Maria Barbara was pregnant.) So now that he can see both 'the possibility of a more adequate living and the achievement of my goal of a well-regulated church music without further vexation', he 'begs' the council 'to content themselves for the time being with the modest services I have rendered to the church and to furnish me at the earliest moment with a gracious dismissal'.

The council acquiesced, apparently with no hard feelings. Bach would maintain friendships with Pastor Eilmar and others; he would continue to oversee the work on the organ to its conclusion; and, as already mentioned, he would compose a new cantata for the council change in 1709 and probably again in 1710.

Bach was the first of his extended family to live and work in Mühlhausen, but he would not be the last. His cousin, Johann Friedrich, succeeded him at St Blasius', and one of his sons, Johann Gottfried Bernhard, became the organist at St Mary's in 1735.

Chapter 5
COURT ORGANIST AND CHAMBER MUSICIAN: WEIMAR (1708–1717)

According to the Obituary, in 1708 Bach travelled to Weimar, where he 'had the opportunity to be heard by the reigning Duke'. This is a bit vague. Did Bach go for some unspecified reason and just happen to be heard by the duke? His request for dismissal from Mühlhausen suggests that he was not searching for a new position. But he always seems to have had his eyes open for new possibilities, and that would be all the more likely at a time like this when Mühlhausen was looking less like a place where he would be able realize his goal of 'a well-regulated church' music. And since Maria Barbara was pregnant, a better income would certainly be desirable. So it would not be surprising if he intentionally found an opportunity to play in Weimar hoping to be heard by the duke, especially since he must have been aware of the age and infirmity of the duke's court organist. However it happened, the duke heard Bach play and offered him the position of court organist and chamber musician.

In July 1708 Bach and Maria Barbara moved into the house of one of the singers in the duke's court capelle (his ensemble of vocal and instrumental musicians). Their home in Weimar, like Bach's childhood home in Eisenach, would be a busy place. Maria Barbara's older, unmarried sister lived in the Bach household until her death in 1729. Other relatives and students would live with them from time to time. Among them was fifteen-year-old Johann Bernard Bach, son of Bach's brother Johann Christoph, who had taken the orphaned Sebastian into his home. In addition, the immediate family grew. Maria Barbara gave birth to their first child, a daughter, around Christmas 1708. She was baptized Catharina Dorothea on 29 December. In all, six of Maria Barbara's children would be born in Weimar. In addition to Catharina, there would be three musically gifted sons – Wilhelm Friedemann born in

November 1710, Carl Philipp Emanuel in March 1714, and Johann Gottfried Bernhard in May 1715. Between Friedemann and Carl, in February 1713, twins were born. Both died during their first month.

The new position in Weimar immediately paid financial dividends. Bach's new salary was almost double his salary at Arnstadt and Mühlhausen. In addition there were substantial emoluments: 18 bushels of wheat; 12 bushels of barley; 4 cords of wood; a 'benevolent entry allowance' upon his arrival; and last but not least, 30 buckets of beer from the castle brewery (tax free). But a greater opportunity to compose church music had to wait. He was hired as an organist and chamber musician. To be sure, as an organist he was involved in church music. But there were two higher ranked musicians, the capellmeister and the vice-capellmeister, who had the main responsibilities for the music in the court chapel. Johann Salomo Drese (1644–1716) had been capellmeister since 1683, two years before Bach was born. Johann Wilhelm Drese (1677–1745), his son, was vice-capellmeister. Bach was certainly aware of this situation before he came, but the elder Drese was old and infirm and the younger Drese was a minor talent at best. So Bach probably thought, not unreasonably, that if he bided his time, a promotion and opportunity for greater involvement in church music would come before long.

Weimar was a small town in the electorate of Saxony. It was the residence of two dukes, who ruled as co-regents. They lived in two palaces connected by a covered walkway, the Wilhelmsburg and the Rote Schloss (Red Palace). The Bachs' residence was in the marketplace near the famous Elephant Hotel (established in 1542 and still operating today). It was within easy walking distance from the palaces. Also in Weimar was the State

View of Weimar showing the
Wilhelmsburg and the covered
walkway to the Rote Schloss.

Church of Sts Peter and Paul, where Johann Walther, Bach's close friend and distant cousin, served as organist.

The two dukes who served as co-regents before Bach came to Weimar were Wilhelm Ernst and his younger brother Johann Ernst III, who had briefly employed 'the lackey Baach' in 1703. Johann Ernst III died in 1707, one year before Bach came to work at Weimar the second time. His son Ernst August succeeded him when he reached the age of majority in 1709. Bach was paid from the joint treasury of the two dukes and therefore was a 'joint servant' of both. But although the two dukes ruled jointly, Wilhelm Ernst was the dominant one. This had been the case when he ruled with his brother who was only two years his junior; it was all the more so when his nephew, twenty years his junior, became co-regent.

Wilhelm Ernst was a stern ruler who imposed a strict, regimented life on his court. Although the name Ernst was common in the ducal family, it

Duke Wilhelm Ernst, ruler of Weimar during Bach's residency.

was especially fitting for this very earnest duke. He was a strict orthodox Lutheran who had studied theology at the Jena University. He made attendance at worship services a high priority for his entire court. He even went so far as to quiz his servants on the sermons preached in the court chapel. The chapel was part of the Wilhelmsburg, Wilhelm Ernst's residence. It had a unique design. Its walls rose up three storeys to a flat ceiling above the 40 × 100-foot (12 × 30-metre) floor. An opening in the ceiling revealed the organ and the space for the musicians, who could be stationed along the balustrade around the opening. Above this was a cupola that reached some 90 feet (27 metres) above the chapel floor. It was painted with clouds and angels to represent heaven (see picture on p. 68). From this symbolic heaven the music emanated. The name of the chapel was *Weg zur Himmelsburg* ('The Way to the Castle of Heaven'). The architecture and the name both indicate what Wilhelm Ernst thought about the function of the space and the worship that took place in it.

Wilhelm Ernst maintained an excellent court capelle, and he recognized and appreciated Bach's exceptional talent. The Obituary mentions 'the pleasure His Grace took in his playing'. So in order to obtain his services, he offered him a salary considerably higher than he had paid his previous organist. In fact, it was equal to the salary of the vice-capellmeister. Later rises would almost double the salary by 1714; and as we shall see, when Bach wanted to take a new job, Wilhelm Ernst would be most reluctant to release him from his service.

The duke was not the only one who admired Bach's organ-playing. His reputation as an organist, already high when he came to Weimar, continued

... all his fingers 'were equally capable of the most perfect accuracy in performance'.

to climb. By all accounts his playing was spectacular. The Obituary says all his fingers 'were equally capable of the most perfect accuracy in performance', and he could play with his feet passages 'which many not unskilful clavier players would find it bitter enough to play with five fingers'. In addition to these technical skills, his imaginative registrations displayed 'each stop according to its character in the greatest perfection'. A visitor to Leipzig in 1729 reported that before he heard Bach, he thought the Italians Frescobaldi and Carissimi represented the apex of keyboard-playing. But after hearing Bach he judged that if they were put together on one side of the scales and Bach on the other, the Italians 'would be lifted straight up into the air'.

Bach's abilities as a sight-reader and improviser were legendary. He liked to claim that he could play any music at sight. So one day a friend (perhaps Gottfried Walther) played a trick on him. He invited Bach to breakfast, but before he arrived he had placed a seemingly simple piece on the harpsichord. Bach, of course, fell for the bait. He went to the harpsichord and began playing while his friend went to prepare breakfast. Soon the initially simple piece turned extremely difficult, and Bach stumbled over a passage intentionally composed to trip him. He stopped and tried it again. After a few failed attempts he finally called out, 'No, one cannot play everything at first sight; it is not possible.' Note that he said 'one', not 'I'. In his opinion (which was probably accurate), if he couldn't play it, no one could!

Given Bach's position as court organist, it comes as no surprise that many of his organ compositions were written in Weimar. Although dating his organ works is fraught with uncertainties, a reasonable estimate would be that about half of them originated during his time in Weimar. These include up to half of the two dozen pieces of the prelude and fugue type. Among them are some of his most widely known and admired works of this type: the 'Dorian' Toccata and Fugue, BWV 538; the Toccata, Adagio, and Fugue in C Major, BWV 564; and the Passacaglia and Fugue in C Minor, BWV 582. But the crown jewel of Bach's Weimar organ works is the collection of chorale preludes called the *Orgelbüchlein* ('Little Organ Book'), BWV 599–644. 'Little' is a misnomer; the only thing little about it is the size of the individual pieces. Most of them are under two minutes long. Some barely reach a minute, but their brevity belies the magnitude of their artistry. They reveal a masterful and imaginative use of a wide variety of styles and techniques. Especially remarkable is Bach's ability to convey the affect of the texts. Albert Schweitzer called the collection 'one of the greatest achievements in music'. 'Here,' he said, 'Bach has realized the ideal of the chorale prelude. Simply by the precision and characteristic quality of the line of the contrapuntal motive he expresses all that has to be said, and so makes clear the relation of the music to the text whose title it bears.'

The *Orgelbüchlein* contains forty-six chorale preludes, almost one-third of Bach's surviving output in this genre. But in Bach's original plan it was to have been even larger. The autograph manuscript contains many pages that are blank except for titles. The titles on the blank pages reveal that Bach had planned to write 164 chorale preludes. The first sixty follow the order the liturgical year; those remaining cover a variety of topics of Christian life and doctrine. Although Bach did not finish the project, it reveals his drive for completeness, a characteristic that will manifest itself throughout his life.

The title page reveals Bach's pedagogical purpose for the collection, a purpose that it will share with many of his subsequent works.

*Little Organ Book, In which a beginner at the organ is given instruction in
developing a chorale in many divers ways, and at the same time in acquiring a
facility in the study of the pedal since in the chorales contained therein the pedal
is treated as wholly obbligato.*

To this Bach added the following couplet:

> *In Praise of the Almighty's will
> And for my neighbour's greater skill.*

It is easy to hear this couplet resonate with Jesus' summary of the Ten
Commandments: Love God and neighbour. Lines from a well-known
chorale, 'Ich ruf zu dir, Herr Jesu Christe' ('I call to you, Lord Jesus Christ'),
similarly resonate with Bach's couplet and Jesus' summary:

> *To live for you,
> To be of use to my neighbour.*

Bach included that chorale in the *Orgelbüchlein*. He also used it as the
last movement of one of his Weimar cantatas, BWV 185. Later he would
compose an entire cantata based Jesus' summary, 'Du sollt Gott, deinen
Herren, lieben' ('You should love God, your Lord'), BWV 77. Bach knew
Jesus' summary well and sought to live it in his vocation as a musician. It
is not fanciful to say that the couplet on the title page of the *Orgelbüchlein*
applies to his complete works; they were all written in the service of God and
neighbour. As he later put it in a harmony textbook, *Precepts and Principles*

Portrait of Antonio Vivaldi (1678–1741). Bach became acquainted with Vivaldi's new concerto style during his time in Weimar.

for Playing the Thorough-Bass, 'the goal of all music should be nothing but the glory of God and the recreation of the mind'.

In Bach's day organists were also harpsichordists, so as composers they usually composed for both instruments. Often there was no clear distinction in style between music written for organ and that written for harpsichord. But in Bach's keyboard works there usually is a clear distinction between organ and harpsichord works, and he was equally adept at writing for both. Since he was a chamber musician as well as a court organist, he had as much opportunity to play the harpsichord as to play the organ. So harpsichord works also figure among his Weimar compositions, but as with the organ works, there are difficulties in dating them. The toccatas (BWV 910–916) were very likely written at Weimar, and it is possible that the *English Suites* (BWV 806–811) had their origins in Weimar, although they were not collected in their final form until later in Cöthen.

Several of Bach's organ and harpsichord works that definitely date from Weimar are not original compositions but arrangements of concertos by contemporary Italian composers, most importantly Vivaldi. There are five arrangements for organ (BWV 592–596) and sixteen for harpsichord (BWV 972–987). These apparently came about through the instigation of a third member of the Weimar ruling family, Prince Johann Ernst, a half-brother of Ernst August. He was a gifted young musician who studied composition with Gottfried Walther. Between 1711 and 1713 he travelled to the Netherlands for music study. In Amsterdam he encountered the practice of transcribing concertos for organ and harpsichord. When he returned to Weimar with many new scores, he inspired both Bach and Walther to make similar transcriptions. Four of Bach's transcriptions are concertos by Johann Ernst, already a fine composer as a teenager. But his life was cut short in 1715 at the age of eighteen.

The importance of Bach's transcriptions is not so much their intrinsic musical value, although they are fine pieces that do transfer successfully from orchestra to keyboard instrument. Rather their importance is due to Bach's encounter with the music of Vivaldi, whose new concerto style would have an immediate and long-lasting influence on his own music. The influence of Vivaldi's concertos on Bach's music extended beyond his concertos to other genres, including what would become the largest part of his entire compositional output, his cantatas.

Composing cantatas, however, was still a negligible part of Bach's activity for nearly the first six years of his employment at Weimar. Three that he probably composed during this time include two fine solo cantatas (BWV 54 and 199) and an early version of Cantata 21, one of his finest. The one cantata that we know for certain was composed during this time is not a church cantata. Cantata 208, 'Was mir behagt, ist nur die muntre Jagd!' ('What pleases me is only the merry hunt!'), was written in 1713 for the birthday of Duke Christian of Weissenfels. It would be revived three years later for the birthday of Duke Ernst August. The subject of the cantata is the hunt, a favourite pastime of Duke Christian. The characters are mythological: Diana, the goddess of woods and the hunt; Endymion, a beautiful young shepherd with whom Diana has fallen in love; and Pan and Pales, god and goddess of flocks and pastures. All sing the praises of the duke. Pales sings the most famous piece from the cantata, 'Schafe können sicher weiden, / Wo ein gutter Hirte wacht!' ('Sheep may safely graze / where a good shepherd watches!') The shepherd, of course, was the duke. Later generations have often extracted the aria from its original context and associated the good shepherd with Jesus, the Good Shepherd (John 10). Bach, no doubt, would have heartily approved.

Bach often took the music of his secular compositions and later provided it with sacred words, sometimes with substantial changes to the music, sometimes with practically none at all. To our knowledge he never did that with 'Sheep may safely graze', but he did do it with two of the other arias from Cantata 208. In Cantata 68, 'Also hat Gott die Welt geliebt' ('God so loved the world'), Bach used the music of two arias from Cantata 208. Pan's aria in Cantata 208 became 'Du bist geboren mir zugut' ('You [Jesus] have been born for my good'), and Pales' second aria became 'Mein gläubiges Herze' ('My believing heart', commonly known in English as 'My heart ever faithful'). In the process of giving new words to Pales' music, Bach made extensive changes. First he took the ostinato bass theme from the original and gave it to a piccolo cello. Then he changed Pales' simple melody into a much livelier melody with exultant leaps, and at the end he added a long, irrepressibly buoyant instrumental conclusion in which oboe and violin join the piccolo cello. The celebration of Jesus' coming into this world called forth much more exuberant joy than the birthday of any duke!

Bach achieved much during his years at Weimar, but for the first six years he was only marginally involved in writing cantatas, the central musical item in a well-regulated church music. But the opportunity, indeed the requirement, to write cantatas on a regular basis would soon arrive.

Chapter 6
CONCERTMASTER: WEIMAR (1714–1717)

I n December 1713 Bach was in Halle. A receipt dated 15 December and signed by Bach gratefully acknowledges the payment of 12 thaler by Our Lady's Church for travel expenses. The church's account book adds that this payment was also for the performance of an audition cantata. In addition the church paid 7 thaler to the keeper of the Inn of the Golden Ring for the expenses 'Mr Pach' had incurred for food, beer, brandy, tobacco, heat, lodging and light.

We do not know why Bach was in Halle; most likely he was supervising work on the expansion of the organ. The organist position had long been held by Friedrich Wilhelm Zachow, Handel's organ teacher. But although Zachow had died in August 1712, the position was still vacant. Whatever the reason for Bach's visit to Halle, while he was there, the pastor, Johann Michael Heineccius, invited him to audition for the position. As part of the audition, Bach submitted a cantata. Cantata 63, with a libretto by Heineccius, and Cantata 21 have been suggested as possible test pieces, but most likely the work he submitted is lost. Bach was verbally offered the position on 13 December. The next day a contract was drawn up but not ratified by the board until 11 January 1714, whereupon it was sent to Bach in Weimar for his expected signature. But instead of signing it, Bach wrote back and said he needed more time because he had not yet received dismissal from the duke's service, and he wanted some changes made with regard to salary and duties. The board was unwilling to renegotiate, so Bach declined the offer. In the meantime Bach had received a raise in Weimar, and on 2 March he was given the title of concertmaster. This newly created position carried with it the responsibility of writing a new cantata once

a month, a duty that would finally put his official responsibilities squarely in line with his goal of a well-regulated church music.

Some in Halle apparently thought Bach had used the offer to leverage the rise and promotion, but Bach strongly denied any wrongdoing. He wrote in a letter that 'the most Honoured *Collegium* applied to me'. He said he would have left Halle immediately after his business was complete were it not for the 'courteous invitation of Dr Heinecke to compose and to perform the piece you know of'. Besides, he wrote, 'I did not need to journey to Halle to have my salary increased', because 'my Gracious Master [Duke Wilhelm Ernst] already shows such graciousness towards my service and art'. Bach's explanation was apparently accepted; at least his decline seems not to have left any ill will. In 1716, upon the completion of the expanded organ, Bach was invited to test and inaugurate the instrument. If the sumptuous menu of the dinner on the occasion of the dedication of the finished organ is any indication, Bach was heartily welcomed.

Back in Weimar, Bach began his new responsibility enthusiastically. On Palm Sunday 1714, he performed the first of the cantatas he would write in his new position as concertmaster, Cantata 182, 'Himmelskönig sei Willkommen' ('King of Heaven, be welcome'). The text was probably written by Salomo Franck, secretary of the ducal consistory, librarian, head of Wilhelm Ernst's extensive coin collection, and a fine poet, who became Bach's favourite librettist while in Weimar. Cantata 182 presents the story

of Jesus' entry into Jerusalem (Matthew 21:1–9) as an allegory of his entry into believers' hearts, and the laying down of garments along his path as the laying down of believing hearts before him. Since Jesus' path leads to the cross, believers pray to him for courage not to flee from 'the banner of your cross'. The penultimate movement expresses the central tenet of their faith in the words of a well-known chorale, 'Jesu, deine Passion / Ist mir lauter Freude' ('Jesus, your Passion is pure joy to me'). It is the reason 'a place is given to us in heaven'. The music must have been especially moving in the Himmelsburg ('Castle of Heaven'), resounding as it did from the heaven-representing cupola high above the worshippers.

For the next three years Bach provided cantatas on a monthly basis for the services in the Himmelsburg. A few of them were re-performances of previously composed works, but most of them were newly composed. The surviving works leave several gaps in the monthly schedule, undoubtedly because some of the works have been lost. Other gaps are due to special

The Ducal Chapel (Himmelsburg) at Weimar, from a painting c. 1660 by Christian Richter.

circumstances such as the official three-month mourning period following Prince Johann Ernst's death, during which no figural music was allowed.

Despite the gaps, the surviving repertory of some twenty cantatas clearly reveals Bach's mastery in what was for him a relatively new genre. As we have already noted, he had very little occasion to write cantatas in his earlier positions, including his first six years at Weimar. Those that he did write were in an older style whose texts came mostly from the Bible and the traditional chorale repertory. Their music did not make use of the new musical styles that came from opera, namely, recitative and aria. In his Weimar cantatas Bach began to use recitative and aria more consistently, but without abandoning scriptural quotations and chorales. It is indicative of Bach's fondness for the traditional chorales that of the thirteen known cantata texts of Salomo Franck that he used, only one does not include a chorale, even though Franck otherwise rarely included chorale texts.

Several of the Weimar cantatas are solo cantatas, that is, they do not use a choir except for simple four-part chorale harmonizations. This is symptomatic of a general characteristic of the Weimar cantatas: they are generally scored on a chamber music scale. The more intimate scale is undoubtedly due to the relatively small dimensions of the Himmelsburg and the gallery from which the musicians performed. Three exceptions are Cantatas 172, 63, and

31, written for Pentecost, Christmas and Easter. For these high holidays the ducal family worshipped with the townsfolk at Sts Peter and Paul's Church. The larger church gave Bach the opportunity to add trumpets, tympani, and woodwinds to the orchestra for those high feast days.

Bach's new responsibilities as concertmaster did not impede his work or reputation as an organist. A well-known story tells of a competition arranged between Bach and Louis Marchand (1669–1732), a French keyboard virtuoso. Marchand was a precocious talent. Already at the age of fourteen he held the post of organist at Nevers Cathedral. Subsequently he held prestigious posts in other French cathedrals. His reputation was so high that in 1708 he was appointed as one of the organists of King Louis XIV without being required to audition. All contemporary accounts agree in praising his virtuosity – and decrying his unsavory character. He had the arrogance and eccentricity that often go with being a 'star'. He also impugned the reputation of other musicians and was unfaithful to his wife. One report says he beat her. After they were separated in 1701, his wife's relentless demands for money may have been the reason he left France in 1713. Another account says his departure was due to an exile imposed by Louis XIV.

Whatever the reason, in 1717 Marchand came to Dresden, where the king of Poland heard him and was so impressed that he offered him a position in his service. Needless to say, Marchand did not endear himself to the court musicians in Dresden. According to the Obituary, the concertmaster, a friend of Bach named Volumier, invited Bach to come to Dresden 'in order to engage in a musical contest for superiority with the haughty Marchand'. Bach accepted the invitation, saying that he would be

Engraved portrait of Louis Marchand, organist to King Louis XIV.

willing to perform any improvisatory task that Marchand would give him, and he expected Marchand to do the same. Marchand accepted, the date and place were set, Bach showed up, but Marchand did not. He had slipped out of town 'by a special coach'.

It seems strange, however, that Marchand would have first accepted the challenge and then simply failed to show up. If he had not felt confident that he could hold his own against Bach, he could have turned down the invitation and invented a plausible reason for needing to leave town. A much later account (1786) might provide an explanation. According to that account Bach was invited by the king to a private recital by Marchand that took place before the scheduled contest. Marchand played, among other things 'a French ditty with many variations, and was much applauded for the art displayed in the variations'. Bach was then invited to play. He accepted, and began by improvising an introduction. Then, to the surprise of everyone, he 'repeated the ditty played by Marchand, and made a dozen variations on it, with new art and in ways that had not been heard before'. If Marchand witnessed such an unplanned demonstration, it is no wonder he had second thoughts and skipped town before the scheduled competition. Bach, on his part, continued to hold Marchand in high regard. His son Carl Philipp Emanuel wrote in a letter: 'Perhaps it will be concluded that Bach was a challenging musical braggart. No, Bach was anything but proud of his qualities and never let anyone feel his superiority. On the contrary, he was uncommonly modest, tolerant, and very polite to other musicians.'

Bach's years in Weimar were good. His reputation as an organist, already high when he came, continued to grow. He was in demand as a teacher as well as a consultant and examiner of new organs. His maturation as a composer of organ music is attested by his *Orgelbüchlein*, a collection of chorale preludes that is rivalled in the history of the genre only by his own later collections. And finally, in his new position as concertmaster, he had the opportunity to compose cantatas on a regular basis. There was a fine poet at the court to provide texts, and the capelle was well supplied with good musicians. Furthermore, he was well paid. Although he still ranked below Capellmeister Drese, his salary now was higher.

But all was not well. Friction between the co-rulers created problems for the musicians. The domineering Wilhelm Ernst was jealous of the music-making that went on in Ernst August's palace, the Rote Schloss. Ernst August was a great lover of music as was his younger brother, the musically gifted Prince Johann Ernst. Both participated in the music-making at the Rote Schloss, which must have been extensive and included town musicians and perhaps students of Bach. The court musicians also participated. But even though they were joint servants of both dukes, Wilhelm Ernst imposed a fine on servants who participated in music-making at the Rote Schloss. As far as we can tell this did not curtail Bach's involvement. He seems to have escaped being fined, but he must have chafed at the arbitrary restrictions on his fellow musicians.

Wilhelm Ernst's jealousy peaked in 1716, when several events showed an especially close musical relationship between Bach and Ernst August. On 24 January Ernst August married Princess Eleonore Wilhelmine of Anhalt-Cöthen, sister of Prince Leopold, Bach's future employer; on 2 April there was a memorial service for Johann Ernst; and later in April and May came the birthdays of both Ernst August and Eleonore Wilhelmine, the new duchess of Weimar. We know that Ernst August's birthday was celebrated with a re-performance of Cantata 208, which Bach had written for the birthday of Duke Christian of Weissenfels. Bach probably wrote cantatas for the other three occasions as well, but the music is lost.

On 1 December 1716, Capellmeister Drese died. The position Bach had been hoping for, and many of whose duties he was already fulfilling, was now open. Perhaps in a bid for the promotion he thought he deserved, he wrote three cantatas in rapid succession for the second, third, and fourth Sundays of Advent, BWV 70a, 186a, and 147a. But when an appointment was not forthcoming, Bach must have realized that the friction between the two dukes made it unlikely that Wilhelm Ernst would ever agree to his appointment to the capellmeister position. In any case, no more Weimar cantatas by Bach survive after Advent 1716. Perhaps they are all lost. More likely, Bach simply stopped writing them because he was convinced his future lay elsewhere.

Chapter 7
CAPELLMEISTER: CÖTHEN (1717–1723)

Prince Leopold of Anhalt-Cöthen (1694–1728) was a music-lover and a talented performer. At the age of twelve his musical talent was already apparent in his bass viol playing. But the Cöthen court capelle left by his father was minimal at best. (Like Bach, Leopold was fatherless at the age of ten.) So the young crown prince prevailed upon his mother, then serving as regent, to hire three Cöthen *Stadtpfeifer* to augment the capelle and provide instrumentalists with whom he could play chamber music. Thus began Leopold's expansion and upgrading of his capelle.

From 1707–1710 Leopold attended the *Ritteracademie* (Knights Academy) in Berlin, a school for young German nobility. After finishing his studies there, he toured Europe, first to the Hague and Amsterdam, then through Germany and France to Venice, and finally to Rome. By the time he returned home in April 1713, he had become accomplished on violin and harpsichord as well as on bass viol. He was also a fine singer.

Leopold continued his efforts to improve the court capelle. An event that happened even before his return home provided the opportunity to take a big step forward. In 1713 Friedrich Wilhelm I of Prussia came to power and disbanded his father's excellent court capelle. Leopold seized the opportunity and again prevailed upon his mother to hire six of the recently unemployed musicians. By 1716 the Cöthen capelle had grown to eighteen fine instrumentalists. Together with town pipers who could be called upon as needed, they formed an ensemble that could rival even those in much larger courts.

Among the members of the capelle was Christian Ferdinand Abel, an outstanding violinist and viol player. He became a close friend of Bach and the godfather of Bach's daughter Sophia Charlotta. The close relationship between the two families continued into the next generation. Abel's son Carl Friedrich, also a viol player, became a student of Bach in Leipzig. He also knew Bach's oldest son, Wilhelm Friedemann, in Dresden. Later he worked with Bach's youngest son, Johann Christian, with whom he presented a series of concerts in London.

One of the musicians who came to Cöthen from the disbanded Prussian capelle was Augustin Reinhard Stricker. He became the capellmeister and was still in that position in 1716 when Leopold reached the age of majority. It was in also 1716 that Leopold's sister married Duke Ernst August in Weimar. If he did not know Bach before, he would have got to know him during the wedding festivities. He met Bach again not long after the wedding at the celebrations of the birthdays of the newly wedded couple. The music-loving prince would certainly have been impressed by a musician of Bach's stature. From Duke Ernst August, his new brother-in-law, he probably heard about the increasing friction between the co-dukes over the musicians and of Bach's unhappiness over being bypassed for the capellmeister position. So he would have known, or at least suspected, that Bach had his eyes open for a new position.

We do not know what happened to Capellmeister Stricker. It is possible that Leopold simply dismissed him to open up the capellmeister position for Bach. However it happened, the position opened up, and Leopold appointed Bach to it on 5 August 1717. But there was a major problem: Duke Wilhelm Ernst refused to dismiss Bach, who in typical fashion seems to have pressed his case for dismissal too vociferously. So the already disgruntled duke resisted Bach's request with a show of power. The court secretary's report says that he arrested Bach on 6 November and confined him to 'the County Judge's place of detention'. He was freed four weeks later 'with notice of his unfavourable discharge'. Many years later Ernst Ludwig Gerber, son of one of Bach's students, wrote that Bach composed *The Well-Tempered Clavier*, Part I, while imprisoned. Although this cannot be true of the whole set of twenty-four preludes and fugues, it is possible that Bach did compose at least some of them or their early versions during that time.

Bach and Maria Barbara, together with their four surviving children, aged two to nine, moved to Cöthen sometime after Bach was discharged. Also with them was Barbara's unmarried sister. Exactly when and how they moved is unknown, as is the location of their house. Bach received rent for rehearsals held in his house, beginning on 10 December 1717. This suggests that their house was quite spacious, large enough to accommodate a family of seven and still have space for rehearsals. If the family had already moved by that time, the move would have to have been squeezed in between the 3rd and the 10th, and Barbara and the children would have to have been busy packing while Bach was still in detention. Since the 10th was the prince's birthday, it is not likely that they moved during the lavish celebrations of that day. And given the tight schedule, it does not seem likely that Bach could have had any significant role in the festivities. Shortly after the birthday, from the 16th to the 18th, Bach had another obligation – testing a new organ at St Paul's Church of Leipzig University. So it is hard to know when they found time to move. But at least by late December the family had moved in, and on 29 December Bach received the first payment towards his new annual salary of 400 thalers, which, with extras, was equal to a little more than double the 250 florins he was making in Weimar. Clearly Prince Leopold was eager to have Bach as his capellmeister. And Bach, for his part, was eager to be done with the wrangles between the co-dukes at Weimar, and to work for a prince who offered him the position he thought he deserved from Wilhelm Ernst.

Cöthen was a small and somewhat provincial town located some 60 miles north of Weimar. It was the first place of employment to bring Bach out of Thuringia, and his position at the court was the first and only one in which he was not professionally involved with the Lutheran Church. Cöthen had become Calvinist in 1596, when the duchy of Anhalt came under Calvinist rule. It remained exclusively Calvinist until 1692, when Prince Emanuel Leberecht rescinded the law that permitted only Calvinist public worship. Not coincidently, 1692 was also the year he married Gisela Agnes, a Lutheran. It was due to her efforts that a Lutheran church was built in Cöthen. It was dedicated in 1699 and named St Agnus's Church. She also financed the building of the Lutheran school that Bach's children would attend.

Leopold, who was the son of Emanuel and Gisela, followed his father and remained a Calvinist. Since Calvinist worship did not involve elaborate polyphonic music, Bach had no duties in the court chapel. So he and his family worshipped at the Lutheran church. But Bach had no musical duties there either. The church had an organist, Christian Ernst Rolle, and a cantor, Johann Caspar Schulze. Bach was on good terms with both of them. He became the godfather of Schulze's daughter. He had access to the Rolle's organ at St Agnus' for practising and teaching; and he probably substituted for Rolle on occasion. Reciprocally, in 1722 Rolle became a member of the court capelle under Capellmeister Bach.

By going to Cöthen, Bach definitely changed the direction of his career. In Arnstadt and Mühlhausen he was primarily an organist, but in Mühlhausen

his interest in choral music grew to the point where he saw cantatas as the musical centrepiece of a church's worship. Then Weimar seemed to offer a better opportunity to pursue that goal, but as it turned out, composing cantatas had to wait. So for six more years his career path remained primarily in organ. But alongside it a new path as chamber musician emerged. When his promotion to concertmaster made composing cantatas one of his regular duties, he launched into the task with enthusiasm, only to abandon it three years later by taking the new position at Calvinist Cöthen, where there would be no opportunity to continue what he had begun in Weimar. He went into his new position knowing its implications regarding his work as a church musician, but at the time he was apparently so relieved to be done with various obstacles he had encountered in his previous positions that he thought he would be happy to work for Leopold permanently. Later in life, in a letter to Georg Erdmann, his old schoolmate in Lüneberg, he reflected on his time in Cöthen: 'There I had a gracious Prince', he wrote, 'who both loved and knew music, and in his service I intended to spend the rest of my life.'

Since Bach was an organist, he was also a harpsichordist. Forkel noted that although the two instruments are closely related to each other, someone who is especially skilled on one is rarely as skilled on the other. He knew of only two exceptions: Bach and his oldest son, Wilhelm Friedemann. Bach also played violin and viola very well. He had got an early start with his father and by now had become very proficient. According to his son Carl Philipp Emanuel, 'he played the violin cleanly and penetratingly', which helped keep the orchestra together. But he especially liked to play viola because from that position in the midst of the orchestra he could best judge the balance of the various parts. Needless to say he had an exceptionally keen ear. Carl wrote that 'he heard even the slightest wrong note even in the largest ensemble'.

Bach obviously had the musical and instrumental skills to lead Leopold's talented capelle, but there is very little among his surviving works to indicate that he had much experience as an instrumental composer (excepting, of course, for the organ) when he came to Cöthen. Some of his harpsichord works originated in Weimar: the toccatas, perhaps some early versions of the *English Suites*, and if Gerber's story about Bach composing during his incarceration is correct, early versions of some preludes and fugues from *The Well-Tempered Clavier*. There are also his keyboard arrangements of Italian concertos, which planted the seeds of concerto writing in his fertile imagination. But the overall picture is very sparse. Beyond a few harpsichord works, composition of instrumental suites, sonatas, and concertos was practically non-existent before Cöthen.

But in Cöthen Bach's composition in those genres flourished despite his relative lack of experience with them. Collections known or strongly suspected to have been written (or completed) in Cöthen are the following:

For harpsichord
15 Two-part Inventions (BWV 772–786)
15 Three-part Sinfonias (BWV 787–801)
6 *English Suites* (BWV 806–811)
6 *French Suites* (BWV 812–817)
The Well-Tempered Clavier, Part I (BWV 846–869)

Solo instrumental music
6 Sonatas and Partitas for Solo Violin (BWV 1001-1006)
6 Suites for Solo Cello (BWV 1007-1012)

Orchestral music
6 Brandenburg Concertos (BWV 1046–1051)

Throughout his life Bach rarely turned out works at the rate typical of other Baroque composers. So it was in Cöthen. Even if we add individual works to this list, for example, the violin concertos and sonatas, the quantity is not astonishing. What is truly astonishing is the quality of these works. At least three of the collections – the solo violin pieces, the solo cello pieces, and the Brandenburg Concertos – are generally recognized as unrivalled examples of their types. Three others – Part I of *The Well-Tempered Clavier* and the two sets of harpsichord suites – are surpassed, if at all, only by later works by Bach himself: Part II of *The Well-Tempered Clavier*, BWV 870–893, and the six partitas (suites) of *Clavier-Übung I*, BWV 825–830.

Two further observations about these works. First, they exhibit Bach's '*summa*' mentality, that is his drive to do something comprehensively, to provide a 'summation', or to bring something to the 'summit' of its development. Second, they show his pedagogical intent. We have already seen both characteristics in the *Orgelbüchlein*.

The Brandenburg Concertos clearly show Bach's *summa* mentality. Collectively they form a comprehensive 'treatise' on Baroque concerto forms and styles. They include solo, grosso, and orchestral types of concerto, sometimes in such a way that it is impossible to label a work as a single type. They unite Italian and French styles, and within the Italian style, Vivaldian and as well as Corellian styles. In instrumentation no two are even remotely alike, and Bach's handling of the basic ritornello form is imaginative beyond compare. There is nothing dry or academic about this 'treatise'. This is music that entertained and refreshed Prince Leopold of Cöthen and Margrave Christian Ludwig of Brandenburg; and it has done the same for music-lovers to the present day. But it is not mere diversion. This is music, to use Bach's words, to 'refresh the spirit' and 'recreate the mind'. Philip Pickett, leader of the New London Consort, likens the six concertos to pageant-wagons in a courtly procession, each one filled with allegorical meaning. Michael Marissen suggests that Bach's elevation of traditionally lowly instruments such as recorder, harpsichord, and viola to higher roles, was a musical allegory of words from the *Magnificat* – 'He has brought down the mighty from their thrones and exalted those of humble estate' – thereby instructing its listeners 'how to think about and spiritually cope with contemporary hierarchies'.

The Well-Tempered Clavier is another of the most obvious examples of Bach's *summa* mentality. It not only contains a prelude and fugue in each of the twenty-four major and minor keys; it also exhibits a seemingly endless

Handwritten dedication of
'Brandenburg Concertos'
to Christian Ludwig,
Margrave of Brandenburg,
24 March 1721.

variety of musical styles and compositional techniques. Even pieces that are in the same basic style and employ the same basic techniques are varied to an extent hardly imaginable. No wonder Robert Schumann advised musicians: 'Let *The Well-Tempered Clavier* be your daily bread. Then you will certainly become a solid musician.' The great cellist Pablo Casals did just that. For many years he started each day playing Bach's preludes and fugues at the piano, but not just for musical training. Like so many players and listeners throughout the generations, Casals experienced them as 'the perfect elixir of youth' that 'refreshes the spirit'; in them he found 'every psychological nuance'.

CAPELLMEISTER: CÖTHEN (1717–1723)

Like the *Orgelbüchlein*, *The Well-Tempered Clavier* is a *summa* that also had a pedagogical purpose. Bach wrote on the title page: 'For the use and profit of musical youth desirous of learning'. Its difficult preludes and fugues were obviously meant for advanced students. But Bach also wrote music for the less advanced. His own teaching took students by steps through the Two-part Inventions, the Sinfonias, and the suites before they were ready for *The Well-Tempered Clavier*. The title page of the Inventions and Sinfonias again clearly reveals Bach's pedagogical purposes, not only for players but also for composers:

Upright instruction wherein lovers of the clavier, and especially those desirous of learning, are shown a clear way not alone (1) to play clearly in two voices but also, after further progress, (2) to deal correctly and well with three obbligato parts; furthermore, at the same time not alone to have good inventions [ideas] but to develop the same well and above all, to arrive at a singing style of playing and at the same time to acquire a strong foretaste of composition.

Bach also made pedagogical collections of his own and other's works for his family. In January 1720 he began the *Clavier-Büchlein* ('Little Clavier Book') for his oldest son, the highly gifted nine-year-old Wilhelm Friedemann.

Chapter 8

DEATH, REMARRIAGE, AND LOOKING FOR A NEW POSITION: CÖTHEN (1718–1723)

The Bach family experienced a rapid succession of joys and sorrows while in Cöthen. One of the joys was seeing the development of the musical talent of the three boys. Wilhelm Friedemann's was already beginning to show when they moved to Cöthen, and during their stay the talent of the younger two, Carl Philipp Emanuel and Johann Gottfried Bernhard, was becoming apparent as well.

Soon after the family moved to Cöthen, Maria Barbara became pregnant again, and on 15 November 1718 Leopold August was born. He was baptized two days later in the Calvinist palace church rather than in the Lutheran church where the Bachs normally worshipped, because his godfathers were Prince Leopold and his younger brother Augustus Ludwig. Standing as godmother was Leopold's sister, the Duchess Eleonore Wilhelmine, wife of Duke Ernst August of Weimar. But the Bachs did not have Leopold August with them long. He died when he was not quite ten months old.

Several other deaths in the family followed in close succession. An aunt died in 1719 and a cousin in 1720. Bach's oldest brother, Johann Christoph, died in 1721; his youngest brother, Johann Jacob, just three years older than himself, died in 1722. The three brothers had lived together after Christoph had taken the younger two into his home after they were orphaned. But the most traumatic death came in July 1720 when Maria Barbara died. In May 1720 Bach had accompanied Leopold to the baths in Carlsbad while an apparently healthy Maria Barbara remained in Cöthen. When Bach returned in July, having received no word of what had happened, Maria Barbara was already dead and buried. We do not know the cause of her death. The Cöthen registry of deaths simply states: '7 July the wife of Mr.

Johann Sebastian Bach, Capellmeister to His Royal Highness the Prince, was buried.' She had been Bach's wife for thirteen years in a marriage that Carl described as blissful. During those thirteen years she bore seven children, three of whom died in infancy.

It is tempting to speculate about Bach's reaction to Maria Barbara's death. The *Chromatic Fantasia and Fugue*, BWV 903, and the incomparable *Ciaccona* from the D Minor Partita for solo violin, BWV 1004/V, have been suggested as Bach's musical response, but there is little credible evidence for either hypothesis. We simply do not know if any of the music Bach wrote in the aftermath of his wife's death is a musical expression of his reaction. So again, as it was with the death of his parents, we know nothing about Bach's emotional reaction, but we do know the theology of death that shaped his reaction, and we know it better through cantatas he had written in the meantime.

As we have seen (Chapter 4), his two earliest masterpieces, Cantatas 4 and 106, provide comfort and even reason for joy for a Christian in the face of death. And more recently, while in Weimar, Bach had written two more cantatas that are relevant in the context of death. Cantata 12 begins with a chorus of lamentation whose music Bach would reuse late in his life for the 'Crucifixus' of the *B Minor Mass*:

> *Weeping, lamenting,*
> *sorrowing, quaking,*
> *anxiety, and need*
> *are the Christian's bread of tears.*

But it ends with one of Bach's favourite chorales, 'Was Gott tut, dass ist wohlgetan' ('What God does, that is rightly done'), a chorale he used in seven cantatas, three of which are entirely based on it (BWV 98, 99, and 100). The verse he used most frequently is the verse used in Cantata 12. It is a profession of trust in God's fatherly care in life and in death.

> *What God does, that is rightly done,*
> *To that will I be cleaving.*
> *Though out upon the cruel road*
> *Need, death and suff'ring drive me,*
> *E'en so will God,*
> *All fatherly,*
> *Within his arms enfold me.*
> *I yield to him, my ruler.*
>
> (TR. Z. PHILIP AMBROSE, ALT.)

Another of Bach's Weimar cantatas is 'Komm du süsse Todesstunde' ('Come, you sweet hour of death'), BWV 161. Its title may sound like a morbid death wish, but in the context there is nothing morbid about it. Bach composed Cantata 161 in 1716 for the Sixteenth Sunday after Trinity. The Gospel lesson for the day was the story of Jesus raising a widow's son from the dead (Luke 7:11–17). Along with the alto soloist, who sings, 'Come, you sweet hour of death', the organ plays the melody of the chorale 'Herzlich tut mich verlangen' (now usually associated with 'O Sacred Head Now Wounded'). Even though the words are not sung, a congregation in Bach's day would have known them well: 'My heart is filled with longing / To pass away in peace.' The cantata ends with the fourth verse of the chorale, which expresses faith that the body, though consumed by worms in the earth, will awaken through Christ, transfigured, shining like the sun in heavenly joy. Of course, none of this implies that Bach did not grieve. But however he grieved, his faith kept him from grieving 'as others do who have no hope' (1 Thessalonians 4:13).

Barely more than a month after Maria Barbara died, the organist at St James's Church in Hamburg died. So in November 1720, probably in quest of a new position, Bach travelled to Hamburg. It is likely that he conducted a performance of Cantata 21 as a test piece. If so, it must have had special poignancy for him so soon after Maria Barbara's death. Its opening chorus is from Psalm 94:19: 'I had much grief in my heart; but your consolations revive my soul.' The first part of the cantata dwells on the grief: 'Sighs, tears, and grief gnaw at my heart', and questions God's presence: 'Why, my God, have you turned away from me in my distress?' In the second part the Soul is still doubting Jesus' presence, but eventually comes to believe and is comforted. The words of Psalm 116:7 – 'Now be at peace again, my soul, for the Lord does good to you' – and two chorale verses are woven together. The chorale, one of Bach's favourites, is 'Wer nur den lieben Gott lässt walten', well known in English as 'If you but trust in God to guide you'. Its key words in this context are 'In the heat of hardship, do not think that you are forsaken by God.'

While in Hamburg, Bach performed on some of the city's fine organs. His performance at St Catherine's Church is particularly noteworthy because he had occasion to play for Johann Adam Reincken, the church's aged and much revered organist. He improvised for almost half an hour on the chorale 'An Wasserflüssen Babylon' ('By the rivers of Babylon'), the same chorale that was the basis for one of Reincken's most famous organ pieces. When Bach finished, Reincken complimented him: 'I thought that this art was dead, but I see that it still lives in you.'

Maria Barbara's death may have caused Bach to look for a new position in Hamburg. To move away from the location of a tragedy is a common human impulse. But apart from that there was another reason why he might have been attracted to the position at St James's Church: it offered an opportunity to return to his goal of a well-regulated church music. At St James's he would have the opportunity to return to the two areas of church music that he had left behind when he moved to Cöthen – organ music and cantatas. In particular he would have been attracted to the magnificent four-manual, sixty-stop organ built by Arp Schnitger. Furthermore, at St James's he would have the opportunity to work with its pastor, Erdmann Neumeister, the pioneer of a new style of cantata text that had become popular around 1700. He was a prolific writer of cantata texts that grew out of his practice of putting into verse his private Sunday afternoon meditations on his morning sermons.

However strong Bach's interest in the St James's position, and despite clearly being the favoured candidate, he withdrew his name from consideration because he was unwilling to participate in the simony that went with obtaining the position. In 1728 Johann Mattheson, a musician and journalist in Hamburg, wrote that a certain great organ virtuoso (Bach) had come to Hamburg and 'aroused universal admiration for his ability'. But the post was obtained by an 'unskilled journeyman who was better at preluding with his money than with his fingers'. This angered everyone

Engraved portrait of Erdmann Neumeister, minister at St James's Church in Hamburg. An important author of cantata texts.

Title page of the Clavier-Büchlein for Bach's second wife, Anna.

including 'the eloquent chief preacher' (Neumeister), who referred to the incident in his Christmas sermon shortly after the new organist was appointed. He closed his sermon by saying that 'even if one of the Angels of Bethlehem should come down from Heaven, one who played divinely and wished to become organist of St James, but had no money, he might just as well fly away again'.

Back in Cöthen Bach resumed his duties for the prince. A year later he remarried. His new wife was Anna Magdalena Wilcke. She was a professional singer who received her musical training from her father, a court trumpeter at Weissenfels, and from an uncle who was the town and court organist at Zeitz. She may have also received training from Pauline Kellner, a famous singer at the Weissenfels court. Her brother, like her father, was a court trumpeter, and her three sisters all married court trumpeters.

We do not know when or where Bach and Anna Magdalena met, but she was in Cöthen in June 1721, perhaps for an audition. Sometime before September, possibly as early as 15 June, she was hired as a chamber musician at the Cöthen court. By 25 September she and Bach must have been engaged, because they stood as godparents for the child of one of Prince Leopold's servants. (Their godson died two weeks later.) On 3 December they were married at home. If Bach's purchase of 264 quarts of Rhine wine from the town-hall cellar is any indication, it must have been a large and festive event, but we know nothing about the wedding ceremony or the festivities that followed.

Anna Magdalena was twenty years old when she married Bach and instantly became the mother of four stepchildren. The oldest, Catharina Dorothea, was thirteen. The three boys – Wilhlem Friedemann, Carl Philipp

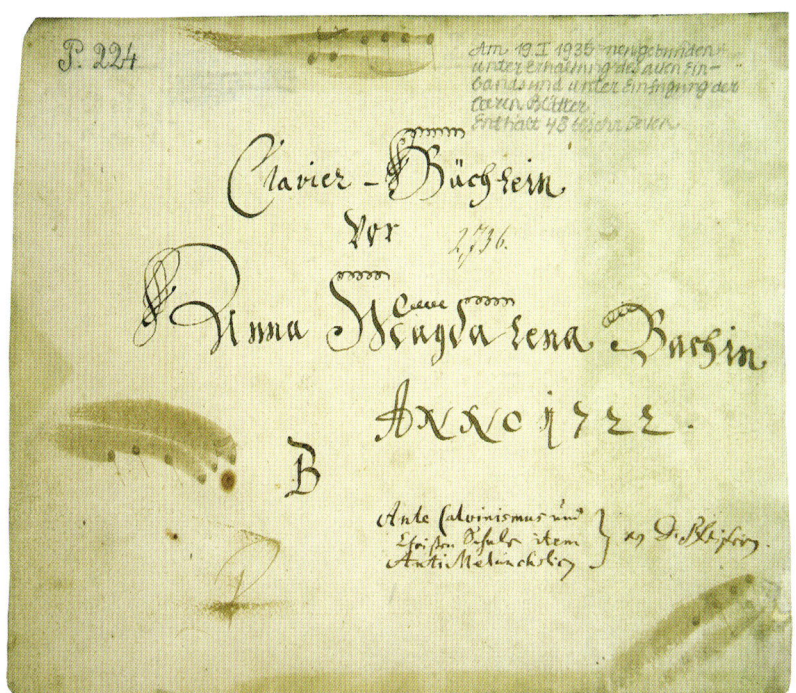

Emanuel, and Johann Gottfried Bernhard – were eleven, seven, and six. Fortunately Bach's sister-in-law and a maid were there to help manage the household.

Marriage did not end Anna Magdalena's recently acquired job in the court capelle. She continued to serve as chamber musician until the family moved to Leipzig in 1723. Not long after the wedding, Bach began the first of two notebooks for his wife. The title page, in her hand, reads: *Clavier-Büchlein* ('Little Clavier Book') *vor Anna Magdalena Bachin, Anno 1722*. It contains, among other pieces by her husband, early versions of five of the *French Suites*, an indication that she was an accomplished harpsichordist. Unfortunately only about a third of the original still exists. Yet along with its companion volume begun in 1725, it gives us a glimpse into the music-making and teaching in the Bach household.

Anna Magdalena had a love for simple, beautiful things like songbirds and flowers. Cousin Johann Elias Bach, a theology student at Leipzig University who served as Bach's secretary, wrote a letter ordering a linnet for her, one that 'made itself heard in particularly agreeable singing'. And in another letter he expressed thanks from her to the sender of a gift of carnations. Elias wrote that Magdalena 'values this unmerited gift more highly than children do their Christmas presents, and tends them with such care as is usually given to children, lest a single one wither'. There is little else we know about Anna Magdalena other than that she was exceptionally fertile. Within a span of nineteen years she would bear thirteen children, twelve of them in fourteen years! Her first child, Christina Sophia Henrietta, was born in Cöthen; the rest were born after the family moved to Leipzig.

Eight days after the marriage of Bach and Anna Magdalena, Prince Leopold also married. This reinforced whatever thoughts Bach might have had about leaving Cöthen. Leopold's wife did not have the love for music that her husband had. Bach referred to her as *amusa* ('without the muse'), but it would be unfair to blame her for the slow attrition of the court capelle that was taking place. Financial problems were also to blame, even before she arrived on the scene; but she certainly did not help the situation. The waning of musical activity in Cöthen may not have been the only reason Bach started looking elsewhere. He and Anna Magdalena may also have been concerned about the quality of education Maria Barbara's children were receiving, and that their future children would receive. The Lutheran school was suffering from shortages of both space and teachers. In addition, the pastor of St Agnus's Church, who was also the school inspector, was a man whose qualifications and character where questionable. So Bach's attention turned to Leipzig when a new opportunity opened up.

Chapter 9
CANDIDATE AND NEW CANTOR: LEIPZIG (1722–1723)

I n the eighteenth century Leipzig was a flourishing city under the rule of the elector of Saxony but directly governed by a town council. Its history can be traced back to an eighth-century settlement at the confluence of the Pleisse, Parthe, and White Elster rivers. By the eleventh century it had grown into a fortified city, and it became an official municipality in 1170. During the sixteenth century it was a flourishing commercial city. The Thirty Years War and a plague in 1680 were devastating, but it made a remarkable recovery and had again become a prosperous city approaching 30,000 inhabitants by Bach's time.

Located at the convergence of trade routes that criss-crossed Europe, business and commerce thrived in Leipzig. It was visually attractive as well as economically prosperous. Due to its many wealthy citizens, the city had many lavish mansions designed by famous architects. It also had pleasant tree-lined promenades, gardens, parks, and coffee houses. Its streets were lighted with lanterns and well patrolled. It was referred to as 'little Paris'. The Leipzig poet Sperontes called it 'Athens-on-the-Pleisse'.

Particularly important to the commerce of Leipzig were the trade fairs held three times a year, each one running for three weeks – the New Year's Fair, the Easter Fair, and the St Michael's Day Fair. Merchants, customers, and itinerant street entertainers came from all over Europe. All kinds of wares were bought and sold: textiles, shoes, paper, jewellery, wigs – even Turkish coffee and American tobacco. A promotional pamphlet of 1725 boasted that Leipzig was where Europe, Asia, Africa, and America brought their 'goods and abundance'.

The book trade was especially important. Even apart from the fairs, Leipzig was known for its book business. Leipzig was also the home of a leading university founded in 1409. The university, the book trade, and the thrice-yearly influx of visitors from far and wide, made Leipzig a cosmopolitan city in which the variety of religious, philosophical, and political ideas that were percolating throughout Europe were available for reading and discussion.

Leipzig was the centre of Orthodox Lutheranism in Saxony. Its Lutheran roots go back to the beginning of the Reformation. In 1519, just two years after Luther posted his Ninety-five Theses on the Wittenburg church door, Leipzig was the location of his famous debate with Johannes von Eck. One of Bach's predecessors at St Thomas's School, Georg Rhau, conducted the choir in St Thomas's Church at the service that opened the debate. Rhau converted to Lutheranism and hence lost his job because at the time Leipzig remained Catholic under Duke George the Bearded. In 1539, after the death of Duke George, Leipzig became Lutheran. On Whitsunday that year, Luther preached in St Thomas's Church. Luther returned to Leipzig many times, including in 1545, when he preached at the inauguration of St Paul's Church, a former Dominican monastery that became the university church.

Leipzig publishers did much to propagate the Reformation by printing many of Luther's writings. The city remained staunchly Lutheran even after the conversions to Catholicism of Elector Friedrich August in 1697 and his successor, Friedrich August II. During that time the anti-ecclesiastical tenor of the Enlightenment was weakening Christian churches of all persuasions, but Leipzig resisted and worship flourished. In 1694 it became necessary to add midweek communion services at St Nicholas's and

Engraving illustrating
leisure time on the Leipzig
Promenade near
St Thomas's Gate in 1777.

St Thomas's Churches. In 1699 the so-called New Church opened. It was a restored Franciscan church that had not been used since the Reformation. St Peter's Church had a similar history of falling into disuse after the Reformation followed by restoration around the turn of the century. And in 1710 St Paul's, which had previously been used exclusively for university functions, was opened for public worship. Add to these the chapel at the orphanage and two churches outside the city walls and it is no wonder that

CANDIDATE AND NEW CANTOR: LEIPZIG (1722–1723)

Leipzig became known as a city of churches. A writer in 1728 summed up this development: 'Until AD 1699 the praise of God was heard in only two churches within the city walls, but now the orthodox believers are taught every Sunday and festival day from six pulpits. In addition, there are two churches outside the gates for the worship of the true God.' The author of the dedication in the 1717 Leipzig hymnal praised the city for its learning and flourishing businesses. But he especially praised its 'well-ordered worship' with its excellent preachers and 'divinely hallowed singing'.

A succession of fine musicians had held the post of cantor in Leipzig since the sixteenth century, including the aforementioned Georg Rhau and Johann Hermann Schein. Bach's immediate predecessor was Johann Kuhnau. He had served St Thomas's Church as organist beginning in 1684 and as cantor from 1701 until his death on 5 June 1722. Bach knew Kuhnau, Leipzig was not far from Cöthen, and its cantor position was an important one in the Lutheran world, so he must have known about Kuhnau's death soon thereafter. But he did not immediately apply for the position. He would write in 1730 that he had intended to spend the rest of his life in the service of Prince Leopold. But that statement might have been more the result of idealized memories than an accurate account of his state of mind some seven years earlier. Still, despite problems at Cöthen, it is not surprising that he hesitated before abandoning his position there. He considered the position of cantor a step down from capellmeister – the change, he wrote, 'did not seem proper'. Why venture back into church music after the contentiousness he had experienced in previous positions? Why work for a town council instead of for a music-loving prince? Why leave a professional court capelle for choirboys and town pipers? In addition to having questions such as these, he must have known

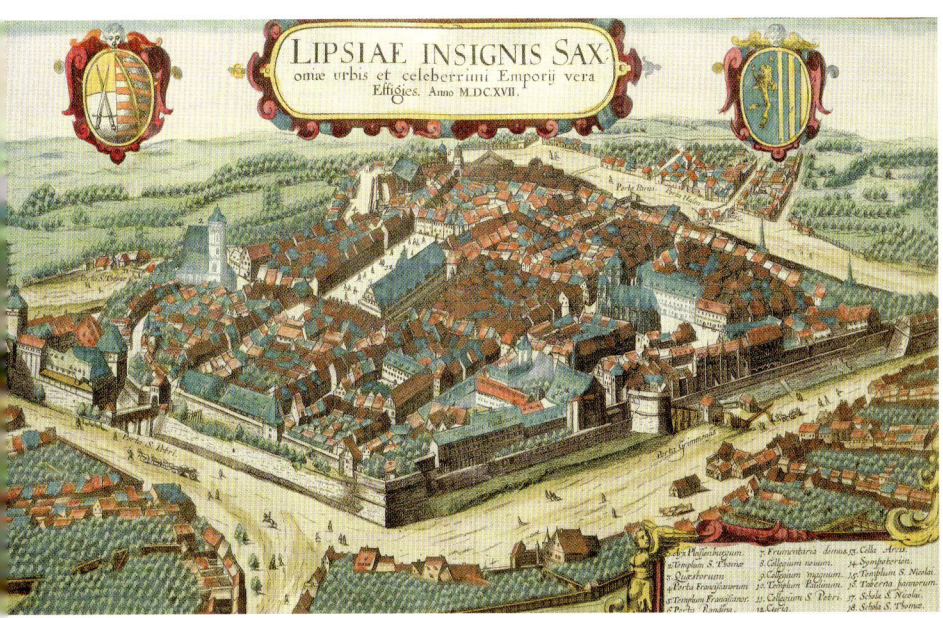

that his good friend Georg Philipp Telemann was a candidate for the position and probably had an inside track. Telemann was well known and respected in Leipzig. He attended Leipzig University, served as organist and music director at the New Church, and founded a *Collegium Musicum*, a group of amateur musicians, often university students, who presented public performances on a regular basis.

Telemann did have an inside track. The Leipzig town council wasted no time in pursuing him. Already on 11 August they offered Telemann the post. But Telemann stalled, and when he finally announced his decision in November, it was to decline. He had negotiated a better offer from his employers in Hamburg.

So the town council needed to go back to work, but the councillors were divided into two factions with differing views regarding the nature of the position. The cantor was both a teacher and a musician. But since the position was primarily lodged in St Thomas's School, not St Thomas's Church, some councillors gave academic qualifications priority over musicianship. Others, however, wanting a first-class musician who could serve as a director of music for the city, thought academic teaching should not be a priority, perhaps not a requirement at all. In Telemann's case the councillors who put greater weight on the academic side of the job went

The great German composer Georg Philipp Telemann (1681–1767) was a friend of Bach and the godfather of his son, Carl Philipp Emanuel.

along with the others, presumably because they realized they could not make a good case in the face of his widespread reputation and musical superiority. He also had a university education in his favour, the lack of which would make Bach a less desirable candidate. The offer the council made to Telemann included a clause that allowed him to hire a substitute to do the academic teaching. But the academically minded councillors were not entirely pleased, and when Telemann declined, they saw an opportunity to find someone who was better qualified as an academic teacher.

There followed a complicated time of debate and political manoeuvring. On 21 December there was still no decision, but it was announced that two other candidates had applied – Capellmeister Christoph Graupner from Darmstadt and Bach. Graupner auditioned on 17 January 1723. By that time the council had already made up its mind to offer him the job. Graupner, though not up to Telemann's calibre, was an excellent musician nonetheless. Further, like Telemann, he was well known in Leipzig. He was an alumnus of St Thomas's School and he had studied law at Leipzig University and music with two of St Thomas's former cantors.

Despite having made their decision to offer the position to Graupner, the council went through with Bach's scheduled audition on 7 February because Graupner still needed to obtain his release from the landgrave of Darmstadt. Bach's audition, like Graupner's, included the performance of two cantatas in a Sunday worship service. He had been given two cantata libretti to set to music, one to be performed before the sermon, the other during communion.

The Gospel lesson for the Sunday on which the cantatas would be performed, was Luke 18:31–43. The passage has two episodes: Jesus telling his disciples that he was going to Jerusalem to die, and Jesus healing a blind beggar. Cantata 22, 'Jesus nahm zu sich die Zwölfe' ('Jesus took the Twelve to himself'), performed before the sermon, begins with the choir and a bass soloist who represents Jesus singing the first words of the Gospel lesson:

Choir: Jesus took the Twelve to himself and said:

Bass: 'See, we are going up to Jerusalem and all that is written of the Son of Man will be accomplished.'

Choir: But they understood none of this and did not know what was said.

The rest of the cantata unfolds the drama of a disciple growing from immature and uncomprehending eagerness to follow Jesus to an understanding that following Jesus means going to Golgotha: the 'old man' must die 'so that the new may live'.

After the sermon, Cantata 23, 'Du wahre Gott und Davids Sohn' ('You true God and David's Son'), was performed during communion. It takes its cue from the second episode in the Gospel lesson: Jesus healing a blind beggar. The beggar represents every one who cries, 'Have mercy!' That cry links the cantata not only to the Gospel story but also to the customary singing of the Latin Agnus Dei during communion, using Luther's German translation, 'Christe, du Lamm Gottes':

> *O Christ, Lamb of God,*
> *who takes away the sin of the world,*
> *have mercy upon us!*

Bach subtly wove the melody of Luther's chorale into the instrumental parts in two of the first three movements. Then, although he had been given only three movements of text, on his own initiative he added a fourth – a splendid setting of the whole chorale.

Both cantatas amply demonstrated Bach's supreme compositional skills, his depth of theological understanding, and his mastery of musical rhetoric. Both works fulfilled their liturgical function admirably, but the added Agnus Dei movement especially showed an exceptional degree of liturgical sensitivity. Since it came at the end of communion on the last Sunday before Lent, it was the last polyphonic music the congregation would hear before Good Friday. 'Thus', as Alfred Dürr put it, 'in compelling solemnity, this uniquely splendid chorale movement points forward to the time when we commemorate the Passion of Christ.'

The excellence of Bach's music did not go unnoticed. Newspapers reported that it was 'amply praised by all knowledgeable persons'. But that is not what got Bach the job. The landgrave in Darmstadt refused to dismiss Graupner, and like Telemann, he received a substantial rise. That left Bach and two other candidates still under consideration. The situation prompted the infamous remark from Councillor Platz: 'Since the best could not be obtained, mediocre ones would have to be accepted.' Bach was the 'mediocre one' they accepted.

On 13 April Prince Leopold granted Bach's request for dismissal. 'We have been pleased', he wrote, 'graciously to grant him [dismissal] and to give him highest recommendation for service elsewhere.' The separation was amicable. The prince allowed Bach to retain his title of capellmeister, and Bach would occasionally return to perform in Cöthen. There were

D. SALOMON DEYLING SS. THEOLOGIÆ PROFESSOR
PRIMARIVS, ECCLESIÆ CATHEDRALIS MISEN CANONICVS,
CONSISTORII LIPSIENSIS ASSESSOR ACADEMIÆ DECEMVIRET
SENIOR AD ÆDEM   D. NICOLAI PASTOR.
NAT. D.XIV. SEPT.   A. MDCLXXVII
OBIIT D.V. AVG.   A. MDCCLV.
AN Æ. TATIS   LXXVIII.

Portrait of Superintendent Salomon Deyling, 1677–1755, theologian of Leipzig.

at least three such occasions before Leopold died in November 1729. Both Bach and Anna Magdalena performed for some unknown occasion in July 1724, and returned in December 1725 for the birthday celebrations of the prince and princess. Bach, apparently without Anna Magdalena, performed again during the 1728 New Year festivities.

On 19 April 1723, Bach signed a preliminary pledge to accept the position in Leipzig. On 5 May he signed a final contract, and on 8 May he passed an oral exam in theology administered by Dr Johann Schmid, a theology professor at Leipzig University, and Dr Salomon Deyling, the superintendent of churches in Leipzig. On 22 May the Bach family arrived with four wagonloads of household goods and moved into a newly renovated apartment in the St Thomas's School. In addition to the parents and the four surviving children of Maria Barbara, the family still included Maria Barbara's unmarried sister. A very recent addition was with them too – a newborn daughter, Christiana Sophia Henrietta, Anna Magdalena's first child. Eight days later, on Sunday 30 May, the First Sunday after Trinity, Bach performed the first of the cantatas he would compose for St Thomas's and St Nicholas's churches. The cantata he wrote for the occasion was 'Die Elenden sollen essen' ('The afflicted shall eat'), BWV 75.

Before moving, Bach had time in Cöthen to plan his first cantatas for Leipzig. He could have started thinking about them as early as mid-April, when he received Prince Leopold's permission to leave. As soon as a starting

date for his employment was set, he would have at least known what the
Scripture readings would be for his first Sunday in the job, even if specific
cantata libretti had not yet been chosen. Whenever it was that he began
thinking ahead to the cantatas he would compose in Leipzig, a note on his
manuscript score of Cantata 75 says that he composed it in Cöthen.

Bach's cantatas functioned as 'musical sermons' in the liturgies of the
churches in Leipzig. They were performed between the Gospel reading and
the spoken sermon. Typically they were based on the Gospel reading. But
the cantata texts do more than preach; they also respond to the preaching.
Bach's task was to write music that would convincingly convey the message,
and that would winsomely and sincerely portray appropriate responses.

The Gospel reading upon which Cantata 75 was based is Jesus' parable
about the rich man and Lazarus, the poor beggar at his gate (Luke 16:19–
31), a story that seems particularly appropriate for the prosperous burghers
of Leipzig. The parable begins: 'There was a rich man who was clothed in
purple.' So in the cantata a soloist representing a preacher asks: 'What
good is the majesty of purple?' He goes on to say that the world's treasures
will all perish. And still worse, worldly wealth, pomp, and pleasure lead to
hell. A soloist representing a believer responds in an aria: 'My Jesus shall be
my all! My purple is his precious blood.' To say that Bach emphasized the
believer's profession of faith would be an understatement. In the opening
section of the aria the soloist sings 'My Jesus shall be my all' no fewer than
thirteen times!

The preacher continues by generalizing from the reversal that Jesus
concretely illustrated in the parable: 'Whoever seeks heaven in this world
will be cursed in the next, but whoever overcomes hell in this world will

19th-century engraving of St Thomas's School which housed the spacious apartment in which the Bach family lived.

rejoice in the next.' The believer responds: 'I take up my sufferings with joy.' And even though there may be 'long misery' in this life, the community of believers, the church, represented by the choir, responds with the chorale 'Was Gott tut, dass ist wohlgetan' ('What God does, that is rightly done').

The climax of the cantata comes in Part II. It relates directly to a sermon by Luther on this parable. He said 'no human being can be pleasing to God unless he believes and loves'. The combination of faith and love needed to 'bear fruit' (as the cantata puts it) is attained in the final aria when the believer sings: 'My heart believes and loves.' The source of that love is Jesus. As a verse from the epistle reading of the day says: 'We love because he first loved us' (1 John 4:19). This is acknowledged in the middle part of the aria:

> *Jesus' sweet flames [of love]*
> *from which mine stem,*
> *engulf me entirely.*

Bach highlighted this theological climax by using the trumpet. At the only other time the trumpet is heard in this cantata, it only plays the simple chorale melody. Here it celebrates the love that flows from faith with virtuosic flourish that prompts an exclamation from the preacher: 'O poverty that no wealth can equal!' And the church responds with a reaffirmation of her faith in God's fatherly care with another verse of 'What God does, that is rightly done'.

Bach followed Cantata 75 with another new cantata the next week, Cantata 76, 'Die Himmel erzählen die Ehre Gott' ('The heavens tell the glory of God'). He had had a reasonable amount of time to compose Cantata 75 before moving to Leipzig. With Cantata 76 he had no such luxury. The manuscript evidence – for example, the number of corrections and the general messiness – shows that Cantata 76 was composed in a very short time, probably three days at the most, so as to leave time to copy parts and rehearse for Sunday. But the shorter amount of time for composing Cantata 76 did not result in a smaller or less profound work.

Bach seems to have conceived the two cantatas as a pair that constituted his inaugural musical sermon to the Leipzig congregations. Not only are they theologically related – the prescribed Scripture readings in the lectionary could account for that – but they are also nearly identical in size and structure. Both cantatas have two parts, one performed before the sermon and one after, and both have the same sequence of fourteen movements, a number that is probably significant. Bach was aware that the sum of the letters of his name is fourteen (B = 2, A = 1, C = 3, and H = 8), so fourteen movements may have been his way of signing these inaugural works and identifying himself with their message. Fourteen may also have signified the centrality of Jesus in the message of the cantatas. Jesus identified himself as 'the Alpha and Omega, the first and the last, the beginning and the end' (Revelation 22:13). In the German alphabet, 'A' and 'O,' the equivalents of Alpha and Omega, were the first and fourteenth letters.

The Gospel reading on which Cantata 76 was based is another of Jesus' parables, the parable of the great banquet (Luke 14:16–24). When all the invited guests excuse themselves from attending, the master tells his servant to go to the city and bring in the poor, blind, and lame; and when that is not enough he says, 'Go to the highways and hedges and compel people to come in.'

Bach wrote a splendid opening chorus featuring a solo trumpet. Its text – 'The heavens tell the glory of God' (Psalm 19:1) – and the splendour of the music might suggest a cantata about the creation or the glories of nature. But that is not the tack that the cantata takes. Rather it focuses on the words that speak of God's revelation of himself to the world:

> *The heavens tell the glory of God,*
> *and the firmament proclaims his handiwork.*

There is no speech or language where one does not hear their voice.

So the preacher concludes, 'God has not left himself without witness.' There is no place where his voice has not been heard. God 'calls through messengers without number'. And then, so as to make the connection with the parable, he calls: 'Arise! Come to my love-feast!'

For his part, Bach wrote music that emphasized the need to hear God's invitation. In the opening chorus he repeatedly placed the greatest musical emphasis on the word 'hear'. Then in the first aria he emphasized the opening phrase of the text, 'Hear God's voice.' The soprano soloist sings the phrase several times, but greater emphasis comes from the instruments. Throughout the entire aria, whatever other words the soprano is singing, the instrumental parts are permeated by the short musical motive that says, 'Hear God's voice.'

But the preacher laments that many do not heed the invitation. Instead they reject Christ; each one worships the 'idol of his own pleasure'. The believer, however, responds that he will reject the world and accept Christ, and at the conclusion of Part I the church prays Martin Luther's chorale paraphrase of Psalm 67, which ends by asking God that 'Jesus Christ's salvation and power will become known to the nations and they will be converted to God'; that is, in the imagery of the parable, that those on the highways and byways will accept the invitation to the heavenly banquet.

Like Part II of Cantata 75, Part II of Cantata 76 brings in a theme from the epistle reading, and again the key ingredient is love. 'We know that we have passed from death into life, because we love the brothers... By this we know love, that he laid down his life for us, and we ought to lay down our lives for the brothers' (1 John 3:14–18). So the believer sings, 'Christ shows me love's sweetness', and prays that 'brotherly faithfulness' may be strengthened. In a final exhortation the preacher sings, 'Love, O Christians, in your deeds.'

Again Bach's ever-fertile musical imagination produced exactly the right music. The gently flowing rhythm of the preacher's final aria is similar to that of the familiar 'Jesu, Joy of Man's Desiring'. It is enhanced by a lovely combination of instruments. One is a type of oboe. Bach often used oboes when the text was about love. In this case the oboe carried an additional connotation of love; it was a relatively new type called oboe d'amore (oboe of love). Bach combined the sound of this new type of oboe with the sound of a nearly antiquated stringed instrument, the viola da gamba, thereby creating a unique tone colour for this theologically key aria.

The final recitative again picks up the theme of witnessing to the world and relates it back to the opening Psalm verse by saying that when the church imitates Christ by showing love, she becomes a 'heaven of godly souls' that 'proclaims God and his praise'. Bach emphasized 'proclaim' – and not just in this recitative. Proclaiming the gospel via weekly 'musical sermons' was now his chief occupation.

Chapter 10
YEARLY CYCLES OF CANTATAS: LEIPZIG (1723–1729)

Composing cantatas and preparing them for performance was not Bach's only task. His title was 'Cantor of St Thomas's School and Director of Music of Leipzig.' St Thomas's was a boarding school for boys. The cantor of the school was responsible for teaching Latin and catechism as well as music, but Bach was given the same option that had been offered to Telemann, namely, that he could hire a substitute for the academic teaching, to be paid from his own salary. Bach immediately exercised that option. That still left an imposing work load. He directed the choir, gave most of the required daily singing lessons (there were typically fifty to sixty boys in the school), and also gave instrumental lessons to the better students. In addition to the music teaching, Bach was responsible for all the music in the four principal churches in Leipzig. Also, he had to provide music for special occasions at St Paul's Church of Leipzig University; and as musical director of the city he was responsible for the music at civic occasions such as the annual change of town council.

To perform the music he had the use of students at St Thomas's School, professional town musicians, and university students. For singing in the churches, the boys were divided into three levels. At the highest level were those who sang the cantatas that were performed

at St Thomas's and St Nicholas's. The middle-level boys performed simpler polyphonic music like motets at the New Church. Finally, the lowest level only sang monophonic chants and chorales at St Peter's Church. Bach directed the first choir; the lower two choirs were directed by older, advanced students whom Bach supervised.

Bach took his teaching and performing responsibilities seriously, but composing was the part of his work that he threw himself into with the most energy. By the time he came to Leipzig the tradition had been established of performing a cantata on alternating Sundays at the churches of St Nicholas and St Thomas. On high feast days the cantata was performed at both churches, at one during the morning service, at the other during the afternoon service.

The magnitude of the creative project Bach set for himself when he came to Leipzig is without parallel in the history of music, perhaps in the history of art. From the outset he undertook the enormous task of composing a new cantata for every Sunday and feast day of the church year, approximately sixty cantatas per year. The Obituary says he wrote five yearly cycles, about 300 cantatas. About 200 of them survive.

These 300 (or even 200) cantatas make them by far the largest part of Bach's compositional output. It is a large number, but it is paltry when compared to the productivity of other Baroque composers. Telemann wrote some 1,700 cantatas, and Graupner wrote over 1,400. But three things make Bach's smaller cantata output more remarkable. First, in scale and weight they far outstrip their shorter and lighter counterparts by the other composers. Second, in depth and subtlety of the rhetorical relationship between music and text, Bach had no peers. Third, the far greater quantity of cantatas by Telemann and Graupner was the result of work over many years. Bach's five yearly cycles were concentrated within no more than seven years. Even if he did not fully complete five cycles, we know he fulfilled his plan for at least two years, and probably for three.

But sheer quantity barely begins to tell the story. The detailed account of Cantatas 75 and 76 in the previous chapter can take us beyond the statistics and at least give us some idea of the rich theological content of the texts that Bach was dealing with week after week, and month after month for three or more years; and with the help of some imagination we can get some idea of how great a compositional challenge it was to set such texts to music.

We can begin by imagining how long it would take simply to copy the score and parts of an average-sized cantata by hand. But then, of course, we need to think about how much more difficult it would be to invent the musical ideas and develop them into fifteen to thirty minutes of music. And those musical ideas could not be invented and worked out in the abstract. They would need to fit the text with regard to prosody, affect, and rhetoric so as to convey the message convincingly. We also need to remember that Bach was inclined towards complex musical forms and styles. Finally, we need to consider that the cantatas that he wrote on a nearly weekly basis were not merely competently done; they were masterfully done in the deepest and fullest sense of that word. Some indication of how masterful they are is implied in the chronology made by Philipp Spitta, Bach's first great biographer. Spitta assumed that most of the cantatas were composed more or less evenly over twenty-some years in Leipzig. He further assumed an 'organic' development that reached a peak in the so-called 'chorale cantatas'. When the true chronology was discovered during the 1950s, we learned that most of the cantatas were written within no more than a seven-year period starting in 1723, and that the chorale cantatas that Spitta regarded as Bach's greatest achievement in the genre were composed week after week during his second year at Leipzig, 1724–1725 – in the midst, we might add, of getting parts copied, rehearsing, teaching, and being husband and father in a busy household!

After composing and performing Cantatas 75 and 76 for the first two Sundays he was in the job, Bach may well have needed to take a break from composing, which he did by re-performing Cantata 21, a Weimar cantata that matches the size and two-part structure of Cantatas 75 and 76. Even if he did not need a break, Bach was probably eager to make Cantata 21 a part of his first yearly cycle. He thought very highly of it and had already re-performed it before coming to Leipzig. He wrote on the score that it was appropriate *per ogni tempo* ('for any occasion'), but its text fits especially well with a verse from the epistle lesson for the day: 'Cast all your anxieties on him, because he cares for you' (1 Peter 5:7).

Bach seems to have written large two-part cantatas like BWV 75 and 76 through the Seventh Sunday after Trinity. (Two are lost, so we cannot be sure.) Also during those seven weeks he performed a reworking of Cantata 147 on 2 July, the feast of the Visitation of Mary. It too is a large, two-part cantata. It is the one that in its reworked form contains one of his most loved pieces, the chorale setting known in English as 'Jesu, Joy of Man's Desiring'.

By the Eighth Sunday after Trinity, Bach abandoned his plan to write large two-part cantatas. For the rest of the yearly cycle he wrote shorter cantatas of five to eight movements. Did he abandon his original, more ambitious plan because the two-part cantatas were too long, perhaps pushing the end of the main service (which started at 7:00 a.m.) too close to the starting time of the noon-time service (which started at 11:30)? Or did he find writing thirty-minute cantatas every Sunday was too taxing? Perhaps, but more likely he found the challenge too taxing for the musicians, especially the choirboys, who were not as capable as he might have thought – or hoped.

In addition to the Sunday cantatas, Bach's first yearly cycle includes eight cantatas for feast days that did not fall on Sunday. Also during the first year he composed and performed a cantata (now lost) for the birthday of Duke Friedrich II of Gotha, tested a new organ at Störmthal and re-performed Cantata 194 at the dedication, and composed and performed Cantata 119, 'Preise, Jerusalem, den Herren' ('Praise the Lord, Jerusalem'), a splendid work for the inauguration of the new Leipzig town council.

Although on occasion there were additional compositional and performance duties beyond the weekly cantatas, there were also two breaks in the weekly routine. Cantatas were not performed in Leipzig during the penitential seasons of Advent (except on the first Sunday) and Lent (except on Good Friday). This gave Bach some extra time to compose music for Christmas, Good Friday, and Easter. So he could hardly relax during those breaks. Each break was followed by the performance of an impressive amount of new music. For Christmas Day he re-performed Cantata 63 at the morning service, but for the afternoon Vespers service he performed his newly composed Magnificat in E Flat, BWV 243a. This is essentially the same piece as his later (and better-known) arrangement, the Magnificat in D, BWV 243. The main difference between the versions is that the E-flat version includes four additional movements with German texts that relate the piece specifically to Christmas. This major new composition was followed in quick succession by six new cantatas for the Sundays and feast days through to the First Sunday after Epiphany, making a total of six cantatas and a sixteen-movement Magnificat within sixteen days! No wonder he repeated an earlier cantata on the Second Sunday after Epiphany before resuming his weekly compositional routine until Lent!

Lent gave him a six-week break from composing and performing cantatas. But at the end of Lent, Good Friday brought with it the biggest chore of the church year – composing and performing a musical setting of the Passion. For his first Good Friday at Leipzig Bach composed his monumental *St John Passion*, BWV 245, some two hours of music telling and meditating upon the story of Jesus' final days of suffering and death.

Since only one day separates Good Friday from Easter Sunday, and since cantatas were also performed on Easter Monday and Easter Tuesday, Bach did not write new cantatas for those days this year. Instead, on Easter Sunday he re-performed a revised version of Cantata 4, and on the next two days he performed parodies. (A parody in this context carries none of the humorous or satirical connotations usually associated with that word. Here a parody is simply a pre-existing composition that has been fitted with new words for a different occasion.) But after the two parodies, Bach composed new cantatas for the six Sundays between Easter and Whitsunday. He also composed a new Ascension Day cantata, 'Wer da gläubet und getauft wird' ('Whoever believes and is baptized'), BWV 37. Then for the three Whitsuntide Sundays and Trinity Sunday he again turned to

From the First Sunday after Trinity to Palm Sunday he composed a new chorale cantata every week.

re-performances and parodies. That gave him a bit of a break from composing before embarking on his second yearly cycle, one that brought with it an additional challenge.

Bach's plan for the second year was to write 'chorale cantatas', that is, cantatas in which the entire text is derived from a chorale. Typically his cantatas had included just one chorale verse in a four-part harmonization as the last movement. In the chorale cantatas, the first and last movements typically use the first and last verses of a chorale verbatim; sometimes an internal movement also uses a verse verbatim. In movements that use the text verbatim, the melody of the chorale is the basis for the music. The first movement is usually a highly elaborate chorale fantasia, and the last is a four-part harmonization with the melody in the soprano part. Internal chorale movements use the melody in a variety of ways, usually in a texture involving a solo voice or two and one or more obbligato instruments. Between these chorale movements are recitatives and arias that paraphrase the text of the remaining verses.

Writing chorale cantatas gave Bach the additional challenge of composing music based on a pre-existing chorale melody. But Bach thrived on challenges. He not only carried out his demanding plan nearly to the end of the year; he did so without resorting to re-performances or parodies. From the First Sunday after Trinity to Palm Sunday he composed a new chorale cantata every week, supervised the preparation of parts for the performers, rehearsed them, and directed the performance on Sunday. In addition he composed a new chorale cantata for each of the ten feast days that did not fall on Sunday. Of course he had the usual breaks from cantata-writing during Advent and Lent, but these only provided some lead time to prepare for the periods of intensified activity that followed. He wrote six new cantatas for services within the two-week period from Christmas through the first Sunday after Epiphany. For Christmas Day, he also wrote the great Sanctus in D, BWV 232/III, which he later incorporated into the *B Minor Mass*.

The last chorale cantata Bach wrote for the second cycle was Cantata 1 based on Philipp Nicolai's chorale 'Wie schön leuchtet der Morgenstern ('How brightly shines the Morning Star'). It was performed on Palm Sunday, but it is not a Palm Sunday cantata. Normally there would have been no cantata on Palm Sunday because it is the last Sunday of Lent. But in 1725 the Feast of the Annunciation, 25 March, fell on that Sunday, so Cantata 1 was intended for the Annunciation.

After the Lenten break Bach re-performed the *St John Passion* on Good Friday, but he replaced or enlarged five of the pieces of the first version. One of the new pieces is a monumental opening chorus based on the chorale 'O Mensch, bewein dein Sünde gross' ('O man, bewail your grievous sin'), which he would later move to the *St Matthew Passion*. He also replaced the original closing movement with an elaborate setting of the chorale 'Christe, du Lamm Gottes' ('Christ, you Lamb of God'), and incorporated the chorale 'Jesu, deine Passion' ('Jesus, your Passion') in one of the three new arias. At this climactic time of the church year, at what will turn out to be the end of his chorale cantata cycle, it is clear that Bach added more chorales to the *St John Passion* to make it fit better into the cycle of chorale cantatas.

Bach's intensive involvement with the chorale is a sign of his conservatism and his efforts to uphold orthodox Lutheran tradition. Because his cantatas are far better known than those of his contemporaries, his use of chorales is often thought to be typical. From the time of Luther until well into the seventeenth century, chorales had been the backbone of Lutheran choral music. But by the end of the seventeenth century that was no longer the case. Alfred Dürr points out that Erdmann Neumeister, the originator of the new style of cantata text around 1700, as well as his successors, 'only with great hesitation [adopted] the chorale in their texts'. The waning of the chorale can also be noticed in the cantatas of Johann Kuhnau, Bach's predecessor in Leipzig. Bach's devotion to chorales was, in Dürr's words, 'decidedly anachronistic'. Despite living at a time when interest in the traditional chorales was waning, almost half of the nearly 1,100 works in the Bach catalogue either are based on chorales or have at least one chorale movement.

Bach's anachronistic love of chorales has another dimension beyond the sheer quantity of chorales and chorale-based works in his catalogue of works. His preference among the chorales was decidedly towards those of the Reformation era, particularly those of Luther himself. Of the chorales used in the cantatas, Luther's account for more than twice as many as those of the second most frequently used author, Paul Gerhardt. Among the chorale cantatas in the second yearly cycle, Luther's chorales form the basis for nine. No other author's chorales were used more than twice.

Given Bach's especially intense focus on the chorale during his second year at Leipzig, it is puzzling that after composing Cantata 1 he composed no chorale cantatas for the rest of the cycle, from Easter to Trinity Sunday. The piece he composed for Easter, the so-called *Easter Oratorio*, BWV 249, is not an oratorio. It is a parody of a secular cantata he had recently written for the court of Weissenfels. After two opening instrumental movements, the Easter story is told in newly written poetic dialogue sung by four soloists representing Mary Magdalene, Mary the mother of James, Peter, and John. It has no chorale movements at all. After Easter Bach kept composing new cantatas for each week through to Trinity Sunday, but none of them were chorale cantatas (though they do end with a chorale verse in a simple four-part harmonization). The most likely explanation for Bach's sudden abandonment of chorale cantatas about two months before finishing the cycle is that he lost his librettist. But since his librettist is unknown, there is no way of proving this theory.

After finishing the second cycle, Bach's cantata production slowed down. Of the five cycles mentioned in the Obituary, the first two have survived nearly intact. A third, which included the *St Matthew Passion*, BWV 244, may have been completed but probably not within one year, and traces of a fourth and a fifth cycle can still be found, but increasing numbers of lost cantatas need to be assumed. The most intriguing possible trace of a lost cycle might be provided by a few cantatas of 1728–1729 on texts by the Leipzig poet Picander, the librettist for the *St Matthew Passion*. He published a cycle of cantata texts in 1728. In the preface he implied that Bach set the texts to music. He wrote that 'the lack of poetic charm might be compensated by the loveliness of the incomparable Capellmeister Mr Bach's music, and that these songs will be sung in the principal churches in devout Leipzig'. But if Bach did set Picander's cycle of cantata texts to music, only a handful of cantatas leave a very faint trace of it.

Bach's slowdown and virtual cessation of cantata composition after 1729 have given rise to many questions. But the chronological discovery of the 1950s that established that almost half of the 200 surviving cantatas had been written during the first two years at Leipzig, and that most of the rest had been written by the end of 1729, does not warrant the radical revision of the traditional picture of Bach proposed by the musicologist Friedrich Blume. He wrote: 'Bach... the creative servant of the Word of God, the staunch Lutheran, is a legend ... [His] numerous works, oratorios, masses, and cantatas ... were not written with the intention of proclaiming the composer's Christian faith, still less a heartfelt need to do so.' To be sure, the view of how Bach carried out his vocation needed some adjustment, but the overwhelming evidence of his life and work still paints the picture of a Christian musician dedicated to using his music for God's glory and his neighbour's good. It is hardly possible to see the almost superhuman effort that Bach expended during his first few years at Leipzig as anything but enthusiasm for pursuing his goal of a well-regulated church music. And although the discovery of the extreme paucity of cantata composition during his last two decades was at first startling, what seems more startling in retrospect is that he sustained the effort as long as he did. Even if everything were going smoothly (which, as we shall see, was not the case), even Bach's enormous creative energy would have eventually reached its limits. Besides, by 1729 he had completed at least two cycles of cantatas for the church. More likely he had completed three, and perhaps as many as five. And since those cycles included two major Passions, he could legitimately think that he had achieved his goal.

Chapter 11

TWO PASSIONS: LEIPZIG (1724–1727)

W hen asked whether the *St Matthew Passion* is the greatest work ever composed, Masaaki Suzuki, conductor of the Bach Collegium Japan, responded affirmatively, but then went on to qualify his answer:

We have done the St Matthew Passion just as part of our series of cantatas. It is an enlarged cantata – you can't really understand what it is without this connection with the others. So in one sense, I don't agree, in that to call it the greatest work ever would be to isolate it as a big work instead of considering it part of the series of Bach's works.

In that same sense neither the cantatas nor the Passions are self-standing artworks. They are part of a bigger whole, namely the yearly cycle. To be sure, the Passions stand out in the yearly cycles, but they do so in the same way that the Passion story stands out in the Gospels. As someone once observed: 'The Gospels are Passion stories preceded by a developed introduction.' The apostle Paul said, 'We preach Christ crucified' (1 Corinthians 1:23). Following him, Luther said, 'The cross only is our theology.' In Bach's preaching, no less than in Paul's and Luther's, the cross is at the centre. It is never far from view in the cantatas; in the Passions it is 'seen' in full, resplendent view.

Bach's Passions belong to a long musical-liturgical tradition. Musical renditions of the Gospel accounts of Christ's final suffering and death have deep roots in Christian worship. Tangible evidence goes back as far as the fourth century, when a Spanish nun named Egeria, while on a pilgrimage to the Holy Land, described the chanting of the Passion story in Jerusalem during Holy Week. The practice of chanting the entire story directly from one of the Gospels spread throughout Christendom during the Middle Ages. During the Renaissance, composers started to set the Passion story in simple harmonizations. Sometimes the entire story was in parts, but more usually the narrative continued to be chanted, and part-singing was reserved for the words spoken by the various groups of people and, sometimes, also for the words spoken by individuals.

After the Reformation the Lutheran Church retained the ancient practice. Luther's friend Johann Walter provided simple models for singing the Passion in which the narration and the words of individuals were chanted and the words of groups were sung to simple recitation formulas harmonized in four parts. This way of rendering the Passion story was still being used in Leipzig during Bach's tenure.

About the middle of the seventeenth century, musical settings of the Passion began to change both textually and musically. The words no longer came directly from the Bible. Instead the story was retold in newly written poetic verse called 'madrigal' texts. Under the influence of opera, chanting and simple part-singing were replaced by recitatives, arias, and choruses accompanied by instruments. By the eighteenth century these 'Passion oratorios' had become quite popular. They no longer maintained the ancient liturgical mooring in the exact words of the Bible; instead they were devotional concert music. Especially popular was a text by Barthold Heinrich Brockes that was set to music by Handel, Telemann, Matheson, and others.

Bach's Passions, however, were liturgical. They are more aptly called 'oratorio Passions'. Despite including madrigalian text, they retain the key ingredient of the ancient liturgical tradition: singing the words of the Passion narrative verbatim from one of the Gospels. In addition to the biblical text and madrigal poetry, they include chorales. The familiar texts and melodies of these congregational songs add to their liturgical fittingness. Both types of non-biblical text function as responses to the various scenes in the story. The madrigal poetry, sung as recitatives and arias by soloists, represents individual responses; the chorales, sung by the choir, represent communal responses. In both cases they draw the contemporary worshippers into the ancient story.

In Leipzig the old style Passions, for example those of Johann Walter, were still sung in Bach's time in the Good Friday morning Eucharist service. The elaborate new style Passions were performed in the Good Friday Vespers service, which began at 1:30 in the afternoon with the singing of a Passion chorale, 'Da Jesu an dem Kreuze stund' ('When Jesus hung on the cross'). The Passion and sermon followed. The Passion, divided into two parts like the larger cantatas, framed the sermon. The service concluded with a motet, the verse and a prayer called the collect, the benediction, and a final chorale.

Oratorio Passions were quite new to Leipzig when Bach came. The first one was by Bach's predecessor, Johann Kuhnau, performed in the New Church in 1717, but the yearly tradition did not begin until 1721, when Kuhnau performed his *St Mark Passion* at the Good Friday Vespers in St Thomas's Church. From that time an oratorio Passion was performed yearly, alternating between St Thomas's and St Nicholas's churches.

Bach's *St John Passion* was first performed at the Good Friday Vespers in 1724, towards the end of his first yearly cycle. It was performed in St

Nicholas's Church even though Bach had sent out announcements that it would be in St Thomas's. He may have been unaware of the tradition of alternating between the two churches – or he may have ignored tradition and announced St Thomas's simply because he preferred performing there. The town council, understandably insisting on keeping the alternation intact, sent out another announcement correcting the location. But since Bach had written the work with St Thomas's specifically in mind, some alterations had to be made to St Nicholas's to accommodate a larger ensemble. Furthermore, the harpsichord at St Nicholas's needed repair. To their credit, the town council took care of both problems. Bach repeated the *St John Passion* with revisions in 1725, this time in St Thomas's Church. The following year, back in St Nicholas's, he performed the *St Mark Passion* by Friedrich Nicolaus Brauns, which he had presumably performed when he was in Weimar. Then in 1727, in St Thomas's, he performed his *St Matthew Passion*, which became known in the Bach family as 'the great Passion'.

The Obituary says that Bach wrote five Passions, but the *St Matthew* and *St John* Passions are the only two that survive. Bach did write at least one more – a *St Mark Passion* which he performed at St Thomas's in 1731, but only its libretto has survived. A *St Luke Passion* that was performed at St Nicholas's in 1730 was once thought to be by Bach (it was even numbered BWV 246), but it is clearly not his work, and it is not likely that it was one of the five the Obituary authors were thinking of.

The loss of three Passions by Bach is certainly a major one, but it is hard to imagine that even Bach himself could have written anything to match, let alone surpass, the two that have survived. Furthermore, the two surviving Passions complement each other beautifully. *St John* is more

TWO PASSIONS: LEIPZIG (1724–1727)

dramatic, whereas *St Matthew* is more meditative and contemplative. The difference in character is a result of the different theological emphasis of the two Gospels. The Gospel of John, and hence the *St John Passion*, view Christ's suffering and death as his victory over sin, death, and the devil. The Gospel of Matthew, and hence the *St Matthew Passion*, view them as his payment of the penalty for sin, the sacrifice of the guiltless for the guilty.

The opening chorus of each work sets the tone. The *St John Passion* begins with words that allude to Psalm 8:1: 'Herr, unser Herrscher, dessen Ruhm in allen Landen herrlich ist!' ('Lord, our master, whose fame in all lands is glorious!'). These words, especially in German with all its 'Herr' ('Lord') words, pick up John's emphasis on the power and majesty of Christ the victor. Bach's music matches the emphasis of the text. A threefold chordal exclamation on 'Herr' is followed by an ascending melody on 'unser Herrscher' ('our master'). The majesty expressed in words and the choir's music is countered by the orchestra. Heavy, throbbing repeated notes in the bass instruments, an incessant, repetitious sixteenth-note figure in the strings, and long, sustained melodic lines full of piercing dissonances in the oboes 'paint' a picture of suffering and grief. This seeming contradiction – majesty and glory set against suffering and grief – is explained in the words that follow: 'Show us through your Passion that you, the true Son of God, at all times, even in the deepest lowliness, have been glorified.' The *St John Passion*, like John's Gospel, portrays a powerful and majestic Lord who conquers sin, death, and the devil, but it recognizes that his glory is manifested 'in his deepest lowliness'. As Luther put it: 'It does a person no good to recognize God in his glory and majesty, unless he recognizes him in the humility and shame of the cross.'

The St John Passion, *like John's Gospel, portrays a powerful and majestic Lord who conquers sin, death, and the devil, but it recognizes that his glory is manifested 'in his deepest lowliness'.*

The *St Matthew Passion* begins with the most monumental of all Bach's choruses. It, like the work it prefaces, is rich in theological themes, but overarching them all it presents Christ, the innocent Lamb of God, out of love dying for guilty sinners. Bach scored the work for two choirs, two orchestras, and a third choir of boy sopranos to sing from St Thomas's Church's so-called 'swallow's nest' gallery opposite the main gallery where the other musicians were stationed.

Leonard Bernstein's description captures some of the drama of the opening. The orchestra 'sets the mood of suffering and pain, preparing for the entrance of the chorus which will sing the agonized sorrow of the faithful'. Together the two choirs sing: 'Come, you daughters, help me lament.'

The resulting richness of all the parts, with the orchestra throbbing beneath, is incomparable.

Then suddenly the chorus breaks into two antiphonal choruses. 'See him!' cries the first one. 'Whom?' asks the second. And the first answers: 'The Bridegroom see. See him!' 'How?' 'So like a Lamb.' And then over against all this questioning and answering and throbbing, the voices of a boys' choir sing out the chorale tune, 'O Lamb of God most Holy', piercing through the worldly pain with the icy-clear truth of redemption.

Further dialogue ensues, urging all who hear to look at the patience of the guiltless Lamb and at their own guilt, each time with the boy's choir soaring above it all with phrases from the chorale. The two choirs conclude with the reason the Lamb died: he did it *out of love.*

Behold him; out of love and graciousness, he is carrying the wood of the cross.

Bach's music for this chorus, like the entire work, is masterful beyond compare. Monumental structure, harmonic intensity, contrapuntal integrity, rhetorical and affective fittingness of music to text, and deep theological understanding all work together to draw listeners into the ancient story, to move them to contemplate and meditate on the suffering and death of Jesus, and to invite a believing response of love, thanksgiving, and service.

We know next to nothing about the response of Bach's congregations. But we can assume negative responses from at least two groups. On one hand there were the adherents to rationalistic, 'natural' theologies; on the other were pietists. The rationalistic theologies sprouting during the Enlightenment would, of course, have been abhorrent to Luther, who once called reason a 'whore'! But he also saw it as a gift of God; he even called it 'the best gift and in a certain sense divine'. He recognized it as a gift that separated humans from all other living beings, a gift that enables them to exercise the lordship over the creation with which God has entrusted them. It provides an essential tool for cultivating the arts, developing the sciences, governing society, and managing all kinds of other cultural pursuits. But his strong language against reason came from his recognition that it is a seductive gift that can lead to man's ruin if it is allowed to trump faith. Since the rationalistic theologies of the Enlightenment succumbed to that danger, it is not surprising that some of Bach's cantatas denounce reason in language that rivals Luther's in vehemence. In Cantata 2, for example, a recitative paraphrasing words from one of Luther's chorales says that those who follow reason 'teach idle, false cunning, which is against God and his truth'. It goes on: 'What their own wit invents stands in place of the Bible.' Against that background it is understandable why Cantata 178 shouts:

> *Be silent, be silent, tottering reason!*
> *Don't say: 'The pious are lost.'*
> *The cross only has given them new birth.*

The apostle Paul said that the cross is 'a stumbling block to Jews and folly to Gentiles' (1 Corinthians 1:23). It certainly was a stumbling block to the Enlightenment. With reason in the vanguard, 'enlightened' Europeans saw themselves as emerging from their 'self-imposed nonage' (as Immanuel Kant memorably put it). Nothing typifies that 'nonage' as much as the cross, and nothing stands so unflinchingly on the side of the 'foolishness' of the cross as the *St Matthew Passion*. The theology of the cross that both Passions proclaim could only be rejected by the adherents of rational theology. They probably did not care for the music either, since Enlightenment aesthetics in general disapproved of complex music and favoured lighter, simpler, more 'natural' styles.

Pietists would have rejected the Passions more for musical than for theological reasons. The pietist pastor Christian Gerber, in 1731, expressed their attitude towards elaborate or 'theatrical' music:

The Passion story, which formerly was sung in such a simple and plain, homely and devotional way, has begun to be presented musically with a variety of instruments and in a most elaborate style, and occasionally a snippet of a

Pages from the autograph score of the *St Matthew Passion*, 1727. They tell the part of Jesus' trial before Pilate leading up to the crowd shouting for Barabbas and calling for Jesus to be crucified.

Passion hymn is introduced at which the whole congregation sings along, and then the instruments again are heard in great numbers. When this Passion music was performed for the first time in one of our great cities, many people were shocked and didn't know what to make of it. In a certain court chapel many honoured government officials and ladies of noble birth were gathered and sang the first Passion hymn with great devotion, but when this theatrical music commenced, all these people were filled with the greatest amazement, looked at one another, and said, 'May God preserve us, children. It's as if a person were at the opera or the theatre.'

Certainly there is much drama in Bach's Passions. But are they 'theatrical'? When he was elected to the Leipzig position, one of the town councillors expressed concern that his music might be too theatrical, and the final pledge to the town council that Bach signed stipulated that his music should 'not make an operatic impression'. Was the councillor's concern justified? Did Bach go back on his pledge? Certainly his use of genres that originated in opera – recitative and aria – gives his Passions (and cantatas as well) a superficial resemblance to opera. But as Christoph Wolff points out, in Bach's music the 'degree of polyphonic elaboration, typical of the church style in general and Bach's artistic preferences in particular, was worlds away from operatic practice'. The centrality of the biblical story,

sung completely and verbatim, and the prominence of chorales also distance the Passions from opera. Regarding the chorale that the boy choir sings in the opening chorus of the *St Matthew Passion*, Wolff says: 'The chorale reverberating from the chancel side of the church warned the audience and alerted the sceptics at the outset that what awaited them was not "theatrical" music, but music that indisputably proclaimed its sacred and liturgical character.' One hopes the councillors heard and were convinced.

It has been said that Gerber's criticism of elaborate Passions was aimed specifically at the *St Matthew Passion*. But the account does not mention Leipzig (just 'one of our great cities'), and it says the work in question was performed in a 'court chapel' (which St Thomas's was not). Further, the *St Matthew Passion* was first performed six years after the Passion performance Gerber was writing about. But even though Gerber could not possibly have been referring to the *St Matthew Passion*, he was certainly expressing a view of music that was not uncommon.

Oh [he wrote], what a blessing it would be in the Christian church, if we still had the simplicity of the first Christians in our services ... If one of those first Christians should rise, visit our assemblies, and hear such a roaring organ together with so many instruments, I do not believe that they would recognize us as Christians and their successors. Of course, I am well aware that I will be subjected to much criticism on account of this statement, but I am well used to that and have not died from it. It is enough that many sensible people are of the same mind with me. I also know that a number of cantors, too, recognize that the loud, vain musical presentations are unedifying and annoying.

Gerber presents a clear picture of the division in the thought about church music in Bach's time. Many would have sided with Gerber. Many, too, would have been among those who thought Gerber and his ilk were 'cranks and melancholy spirits or ill-humoured' (Gerber's words). But even among this latter group there were probably not many who fully recognized the surpassing greatness that posterity continues to hear in Bach's two surviving Passions.

Bach performed the *St John Passion* at least four times, the last time in 1749. Each time he made revisions, but given the scores and parts that have survived, it is not possible to ascertain his final intentions. The situation is different with the *St Matthew Passion*. He performed it three or four times, but revised it only once, in 1736. He was apparently satisfied that the 1736 version was as good as he could make it. He made a beautiful fair copy of the score, even taking the trouble to write all the words from the Bible in red ink (see picture on p. 128).

Chapter 12
PROBLEMS AND NEW PROJECTS: LEIPZIG (1727–1734)

However complete or incomplete the five yearly cycles of cantatas and Passions were in 1729, Bach may have been satisfied that he had a sufficient stock for a well-regulated church music. But satisfaction seems an unlikely explanation for his near cessation of cantata composition. At least it is an insufficient explanation. Other factors played a role. His workload, even without composition, was heavy. He still had his daily school duties and weekly church performances. He still taught private students, was consulted about new organs, tested them when finished, and made guest appearances as a performer. Beyond the usual busyness there were difficulties both at work and at home that must have taxed his time, his energy, and even his incentive.

At home the steady succession of births and deaths had to take an emotional toll. Of course, dealing with deaths in the immediate family was nothing new to Bach. He had faced it before he reached his tenth birthday, when both of his parents died within a year of each other. He had faced it again when his first wife and three of their seven children died. But the rollercoaster ride of joy in birth and sorrow in death accelerated in Leipzig. Counting the daughter born just before moving to Leipzig, there were thirteen births within nineteen years, twelve of them in fourteen years. Six children were born to Anna Magdalena in six consecutive years from 1723 to 1728. But in 1726 her first child, aged three, died, and in 1727 a son died the day after his baptism. In the decade from 1728 to 1737 there were only three years in which she did not give birth, and during the same timespan she saw the deaths of five more of her children. During a six-year period from 30 October 1727, to 6 November 1733, she bore six children and buried six children. Only six of her thirteen children

Copper engraving of poet Johann Christoph Gottsched, 1700–1766, by J. M. Bernigeroth, based on a painting by Johann Friedrich Reiffenstein, 1757.

lived into adulthood and outlived their mother. One of them was Gottfried Heinrich, her oldest son. He had a learning disability that prevented him from attending St Thomas's School; he needed to be schooled at home.

At work there were problems with colleagues and superiors. A commission Bach received in the autumn of 1727, about half a year after the first performance of the *St Matthew Passion*, resulted in a skirmish with a colleague. Although the problem was petty, it was symptomatic. The commission was for music for a memorial service for Christiane Eberhardine, electress of Saxony and queen of Poland. She was the wife of Friedrich August I, but when her husband converted to Catholicism for political reasons, she separated from him and remained Lutheran. For her loyalty to the Lutheran faith she was dearly loved throughout Saxony. An official four-month period of mourning was declared. Among the commemorative events was a memorial service in Leipzig at St Paul's, the university church. A student commissioned the eminent poet Johann Christoph Gottsched to write an ode of mourning for the occasion; Bach was to set it to music. Bach's involvement resulted in a 'turf war' (not the first) with the director of music at St Paul's, Johann Gottlieb Görner. Görner was miffed that Bach was chosen to compose the music for Gottsched's ode. He saw it as an infringement on his official rights. He tried to get Bach to sign a statement saying that he recognized that the commission was a favour, and that it was not to set a precedent. Further, Bach was never to claim the directorship of music at St Paul's or to contract to provide music for other occasions without permission of the university. Bach refused to sign, Görner was paid 12 thalers, and Bach's music was performed.

More critical than this kind of occasional run-in with a colleague were problems with music in the church, in particular with the performance of cantatas. The problems must have been building for some time, causing frustrations that came to a head in 1730 when Bach sent a memo to the Leipzig town council titled 'Short but Most Necessary Draft for a Well-Appointed Church Music'. In it Bach complained about the lack of resources needed to meet minimum standards for performing cantatas. The ability of the students in the choir was declining due to lowered musical standards for admission. Further, eight town pipers and professional fiddlers were the only instrumentalists currently appointed, but at least eighteen were required. Formerly the difference was made up by university students, but since they were no longer paid, it was difficult to enlist their services. The result was a decline that had reached a critically low level. Response from the council, if there was any, has not survived. Two months after sending the memo, Bach wrote to his boyhood friend Georg Erdmann seeking help in finding another position. In it he described the Leipzig authorities as 'odd and little interested in music, so that I must live amid almost continual vexation, envy, and persecution'.

Frustration with this situation undoubtedly played a role in the slowdown and near cessation of Bach's cantata production. But although church cantatas became a very small part of his compositional output after 1729, he did not entirely neglect them. He wrote some new cantatas to fill gaps in the yearly cycles, especially for the cycle of chorale cantatas. Some gaps were due to the fact that the date of Easter moves, which makes the length of the Epiphany and Trinity seasons vary from year to year. One of his best-known cantatas, 'Wachet auf, ruft uns die Stimme' ('Wake, awake, for night is flying'), BWV 140, was written in 1731 for the Twenty-seventh Sunday after Trinity, a Sunday that occurs only when Easter is very early. The year 1731 was the first in which it happened during Bach's time in Leipzig. Gaps also occurred when a special feast day came on a Sunday. For example, in 1724 the Feast of the Visitation occurred on the Fourth Sunday after Trinity, so that year Bach had composed a Visitation cantata instead of a cantata for the Fourth Sunday after Trinity. In 1732 he filled that gap by composing Cantata 177, 'Ich ruf zu dir, Herr Jesu Christ' ('I call to you, Lord Jesu Christ').

Bach also continued to write new cantatas for special occasions such as weddings, funerals, and changes of the town council. Given the 'continuous vexation' Bach received from the town officials, one might wonder how much effort he put into his cantatas for the council change. Cantata 29, 'Wir danken dir Gott' ('We thank you, God'), written in 1731, gives the answer: Bach wrote the best music he could for the occasion regardless of his personal feelings towards those being honoured. Cantata 29 begins with an instrumental sinfonia that is built on the brilliant prelude from the E Major Partita for unaccompanied violin, BWV 1006/I. But in starting with a pre-existing piece, Bach was not taking a shortcut. Instead, he made a brilliant piece even more brilliant. He gave the violin's continuous rush of sixteenth-notes to the organ and punctuated it with chords and fanfare motives featuring the trumpets and timpani. The opening chorus is equally splendid but in a very different way. Its splendour derives from the fugal development of a quiet, serene theme rather than from virtuosity and fanfares. Bach thought so highly of it that he re-used it in the *B Minor Mass* – not once but twice!

Several of Bach's late cantatas are chorale cantatas, an indication of his continuing fondness for chorales, the venerable congregational hymns of his church. The late chorale cantatas differ from those of the second yearly cycle in that they use the words of all the verses verbatim instead of having some of the verses summarized in newly composed poetry. In addition to the late chorale cantatas that fill gaps in the second cycle, there are four based on chorales specified for weddings. One of them is Cantata 100, 'Was Gott tut, dass ist wohlgetan' ('What God does, that is rightly done'), the third of Bach's cantatas based on that beloved expression of trust in God.

Since his cantata composition had become such a minimal part of his activities, Bach had time for other pursuits. Among them was a return to composing for organ and harpsichord. During the late 1720s and early 1730s he composed a few works that must be numbered among his greatest organ works: the six trio sonatas, BWV 525–530, and the preludes and fugues in B minor (BWV 544), C minor (BWV 546), and E minor (BWV 548). He also composed six partitas (or suites) for harpsichord which was the beginning of a new venture for him – publication. Until now his only work that had been published was the Mühlhausen cantata, 'Gott ist mein König' ('God is my King', BWV 71), and that was done at the town council's initiative, not Bach's. But in 1731 the six partitas were published together in a collection titled *Clavier-Übung* ('Keyboard Practice'), BWV 825–830. This was the first of four collections of keyboard music he would publish during the next ten years, all under that title.

Bach also added another activity to his schedule. In 1729 he became the director of a *Collegium Musicum*. There were two such organizations in Leipzig while Bach was there. The one Bach directed, which performed at Zimmermann's Coffee House, was founded by Telemann in 1702. In winter they performed in the coffee house every Friday from 8:00 to 10:00 p.m. and in summer in the coffee garden on Wednesday afternoons. During fairs they performed twice a week on Tuesday and Friday evenings. Bach continued as director into the early 1740s with the exception of a two-year break from 1737 to 1739.

There is no record of what music was performed at the concerts. Some of Bach's secular cantatas were probably performed. His *Coffee Cantata*, BWV 211, humorously based on the new craze for coffee, would have been especially appropriate for a performance at Zimmermann's. But vocal music was probably less frequent than instrumental sonatas, suites, and concertos. Most of the music was probably by composers other than Bach, although he certainly would have performed his own works as well. Any of his chamber and orchestral music from Leipzig, as well as earlier music from Weimar and

Bach's *Collegium Musicum* performed in Zimmermann's Coffee House located on Catharinenstrasse, a main street off Market Square in Leipzig.

Bach's eldest son, Wilhelm Friedemann, 1710–1784.

Cöthen, could have been performed at Zimmermann's. We can assume he wrote pieces for the *Collegium Musicum* that have been lost. We are quite certain that his harpsichord concertos, BWV 1052–1065, were made specifically for his *Collegium Musicum* performances. Almost all of them are arrangements of his earlier concertos for other instruments; they may have been made to feature his sons, his students, and himself as soloists.

His oldest sons were now ready for university and musical careers. Wilhelm Friedemann and Carl Philipp Emanuel matriculated at Leipzig University in 1729 and 1731 respectively. In 1733 Friedemann was appointed organist at St Sophia's Church in Dresden. A year later, Carl matriculated at the University of Frankfurt-on-the-Oder. The third oldest son, Johann Gottfried Bernhard, did not immediately go to university. After graduating from St Thomas's School he went directly into a music career. Thanks at least in part to his father's connections, Gottfried was appointed to the organist post at St Mary's Church in Mühlhausen in 1735.

Bach himself may have been thinking about a new position again too. The council was not addressing the complaints outlined in his 1730 memo. The council, for its part, had complaints about Bach pertaining to teaching and following regulations. Although it is impossible to ascertain the exact nature of the complaints or their validity, there can be little doubt that Bach was not always without fault. What is abundantly clear is that the two parties were unhappy with each other. There was a lot of sniping back and forth and little co-operation. But out of this contentious situation came one of Bach's greatest works, a work that he submitted along with an application for a prestigious title that he thought would give him more clout in Leipzig.

Bach's second son,
Carl Philipp Emanuel,
1714–1788.

Augustus the Strong, king of Poland and elector of Saxony, had died on 1 February 1733. During the period of mourning that followed, no figural music was performed in the churches, so Bach was free from the duties of preparing cantatas and a Passion for performance that spring. During that time he wrote his magnificent *Missa* (BWV 232/I), which later became the Kyrie and Gloria of the *B Minor Mass*. On 27 July 1733 he delivered a petition to Augustus' son and successor, Elector Friedrich Augustus II (King Augustus III). In it he frankly admitted the reason for his petition:

For some years and up to the present moment, I have had the Directorium of the Music in the two principal churches in Leipzig, but have innocently had to suffer one injury and another, and on occasion also a diminution of the fees accruing to me in this office; but these injuries would disappear altogether if Your Royal Highness would grant me the favour of conferring upon me a title of Your Royal Highness's Court Capelle.

Accompanying the petition was the *Missa*. Never, it is safe to say, has a job or title application been accompanied by so much evidence of the applicant's qualifications, evidence that Bach called 'a small work of that science which I have achieved in *musique*'! He hoped it would be looked upon 'with Most Gracious Eyes, according to Your Highness's World-Famous Clemency and not according to the poor *composition*'. Three years later the king finally got round to acting on Bach's application. He issued a certificate saying that he 'has most graciously conferred upon Johann Sebastian Bach, on the latter's most humble entreaty and because of his ability, the title of *Compositeur to the Royal Court Orchestra*'.

Johann August Ernesti, rector of St Thomas's School, 1734–1759.

A year after composing the *Missa*, Bach became embroiled in another controversy. This one was with the newly appointed rector of St Thomas's School, Johann August Ernesti. The conflict is known to us from a long, unedifying series of complaints and rebuttals sent to the town council by both parties. At issue was the right to appoint a student prefect. In other words it was another turf war. But this one was not a minor skirmish. The combatants became bitter enemies. Ernesti was no lover of music. He held a low view of music typical of the Enlightenment. Therefore he resented its place in St Thomas's curriculum because it took time away from academic study that he deemed more valuable. He not only sought to diminish music's place in the curriculum; he also discouraged students from pursuing their musical studies. To a student practising violin he said derisively, 'So you want to become a beer-fiddler too?'

At bottom something far more serious than turf was at stake. Theologian Paul Minear did not overstate the case when he wrote: 'Two epochs, two cultures, two philosophies of education were at stake. Should secondary education continue to be grounded in Christian theology? If so, should music be given a central place in such training?' As Leo Schrade put it: 'With Ernesti as the rector of St Thomas's, the old principle of the school, "to guide the students through the euphony of music to the contemplation of the divine", was discarded.' At bottom the conflict was a cultural one between the waning Age of Faith and the waxing Age of Enlightenment.

Chapter 13
CONTINUING PROBLEMS AND PROJECTS: LEIPZIG (1734–1739)

At the deepest level, the cultural clash was religious. The theology of Bach's cantatas and Passions, based on God's revealed Word in the Bible and centred on Christ's redeeming death, stood against the Enlightenment's 'natural' theology centred on common-sense morality and an optimistic view of human nature. But the clash was also aesthetic. Returning for a moment to Bach's involvement in Christiane Eberhardine's memorial service, we can find an interesting confrontation of aesthetic values.

The product of the Bach/Gottsched collaboration is a splendid work now numbered among Bach's cantatas as BWV 198. It is not likely that Gottsched, a leading figure in the German Enlightenment, would have been pleased with Bach's music. One of Gottsched's literary rules was that genres should be clearly distinguished. So the ode that he wrote for Christiane Eberhardine's memorial service is in conformity with his criteria for the structure of odes. It consists of nine eight-line strophes, each with an ABBA/CDDC pattern of rhymes. For example, here is the second strophe:

Hier klagt August und Prinz und Land,	*A*
Der Adel ächzt, der Bürger trauert,	*B*
Wie hat dich nicht das Volk bedauert,	*B*
Sobald es deinen Fall empfand!	*A*
Verstummt! verstummt, ihr holden Saiten!	*C*
Kein Ton ermag der Länder Not	*D*
Bei ihrer teuren Mutter Tod,	*D*
O Schmerzenswort! recht anzudeuten.	*C*

The title page of *Clavier-Übung,*
Part II, published in 1735.

Zweyter Theil
Der
Clavier Übung
bestehend in

einem Concerto *nach Italiænischen Gusto*
und

einer Overture *nach Französischer Art.*

vor ein

Clavicymbel mit zweyen
Manualen.

Denen Liebhabern zur Gemüths-Ergötzung verfertiget
von

Johann Sebastian Bach.
Hochfürstl. Sæchsl. Weißenfelsl. Capellmeistern
und

Directore Chori Musici Lipsiensis.
in Verlegung
Christoph *Weigel* *Junioris.*

But Bach showed little respect for the structure of Gottsched's ode. His music breaks up and reorders Gottsched's nine rigidly structured strophes into ten movements. Furthermore, the use of recitatives and arias was at odds with Gottsched's dislike for what he considered to be Italian excesses. Instead of the 'noble simplicity' that he required, he got from Bach what his student Johann Adolph Scheibe called 'excessive art and unnatural contrivance'. The Enlightenment stressed 'Nature' (always the capital 'N' version) over 'art'. 'True art', wrote Scheibe, 'always seeks that which is natural. Nature need borrow no rouge from art.' According to Scheibe and Enlightenment thought in general, not to follow Nature – or conversely, to indulge in an excess of art – leads to disorder, bombast, obscurity, and confusion.

Bach's music blatantly went counter to Gottsched's aesthetic ideas, but if the latter had objections they have left no trace. He had not entered into this collaboration unaware of what Bach's music was like. He worshipped regularly at St Thomas's Church, and he had collaborated with Bach before (and would again). He even wrote in 1728 that Bach was 'head and shoulders above his peers', and in 1732 he sent Bach's recently published harpsichord partitas, *Clavier-Übung I*, to his fiancée. Did Gottsched not recognize the dissonance between his aesthetic ideas and Bach's? Or did he simply tolerate Bach's music because he recognized greatness in Bach's music, even though it ran counter to his aesthetic theories? Perhaps he even liked Bach's music? We do not know.

Bach's compositional activity during the mid- and late 1730s continued the projects he began in the late 1720s. In 1735 he published a second *Clavier-Übung* volume. It contains the Italian Concerto, BWV 971, and the Ouverture in the French Style, BWV 831. In these works Bach took the two principal orchestral genres in the two predominant national styles of the time and transferred them to the two-manual harpsichord. Also, in the Italian Concerto, he demonstrated that he could write music that satisfied Enlightenment tastes. Even Scheibe, who would become Bach's most famous Enlightenment critic, called it 'a perfect model of a well-designed concerto'.

In addition to continuing his project of publishing keyboard works, Bach continued to fill gaps in his output of liturgical music. In the previous chapter we noted his filling gaps in his cantata cycles. The mid- and late 1730s saw him active in two other areas of liturgical music, *historiae* and the Mass.

A *historia* is a musical setting of the biblical account of Jesus' birth, death, resurrection, or ascension. Bach's Passions are *historiae*. So his activity in that genre during the 1730s includes composing the lost *St Mark Passion* (1731), making his final, definitive version of the *St Matthew Passion* in 1736, and the revisions to the *St John Passion* in 1732 and 1739. Also included among the *historiae* are the *Ascension Oratorio*, BWV 11, and the *Christmas Oratorio*, BWV 248. (The *Easter Oratorio* is not a *historia*. See Chapter 10.) The *Ascension Oratorio* was written in 1735. In the catalogue of Bach's works it is numbered among the cantatas, probably because it is cantata-like in size. But it is a true oratorio, or *historia*, built around the biblical account, which is sung, as in the Passions, in recitative style. Its brevity in comparison with the Passions and the *Christmas Oratorio* is simply the result of the brevity of the story, a mere six verses taken from Luke, Mark, and Acts.

In magnitude the *Christmas Oratorio* belongs with the two Passions and the *B Minor Mass*. It was first performed between Christmas and Epiphany 1734–1735. It has six distinct parts to be performed on six separate occasions: the First, Second, and Third Days of Christmas, the Feast of Circumcision, the First Sunday in the New Year, and the Feast of Epiphany. Each part can stand alone as a separate piece of cantata-like proportions. Parts I–III tell the story of Christ's birth from Luke 2:1–20; Part IV tells of his circumcision from Luke 2:21, and Parts V and VI tell of the visit of the Wise Men from Matthew 2:1–12. Each part is a cantata-sized work framed by choruses, and as in the Passions, the biblical story, sung verbatim from the Gospels, is interspersed with responses in the form of recitatives, arias, and chorales. Despite being intended for performance on six different days, Bach called the six parts collectively an oratorio. He never performed any part of it separately from the other parts during a given Christmas/Epiphany season. Of course the continuity of the story holds the six parts together, but Bach also took considerable care musically to unify and give coherent shape to the six parts together, particularly in instrumentation and succession of keys.

The *Christmas Oratorio*, like many of Bach's works from the 1730s and 1740s, contains much parody. But as we have noted before, that should not be taken as a sign of second-class work. Bach was neither resorting to parody to save time – being free from weekly composition of cantatas, he had ample time to compose new works – nor resorting to it because his creative powers were failing. The new works from the 1730s and 1740s give ample evidence that he retained his unparalleled compositional skill and imagination to the end.

So, then, why parodies? Since his parodies usually turn secular works into liturgical works, it seems that he saw parody as a way to prevent some of his finer secular works from falling into disuse, and to put them to better use. For example, by the time he began to compose the *Christmas Oratorio* he had already lavished a great deal of art on secular cantatas to celebrate the birthdays of various dukes and princes. Why not give that music more chances to be heard by more people? And more importantly, why not let that splendid music serve to celebrate the birth of the King of Kings rather than limit it to the birthdays of minor German dukes or princes?

Bach's two new *historiae* augmented his well-ordered church music. So did his *missae* (Kyrie and Gloria). In Leipzig during Bach's time it was customary to perform figural Latin *missae* on high feast days. In the late 1730s Bach wrote four *Missae breves*, BWV 233–236. These works are largely parodies, their music derived from Bach's own cantatas.

In 1737 the aforementioned Johann Adolph Scheibe published the most famous criticism of Bach's music. It appeared in *Critische Musikus*, a music journal Scheibe founded in Hamburg. He praised Bach as 'an extraordinary artist' on harpsichord and organ, but criticized his compositions for their lack of 'amenity'. They are overly ornate, he wrote, 'turgid' and 'confused', their beauty darkened 'by an excess of art'. From the point of view of an Enlightenment aesthetic that valued what is simple, uncomplicated, and direct, Scheibe's criticism is right on target. To that way of thinking Bach's 'learned' music is 'artificial' and thus in conflict with 'Nature'.

Bach may have been stung by Scheibe's criticism; some of his supporters sprang to his defence in print. But stung or not, he would not have been moved by the idea that his music was in conflict with nature; he would have denied the accusation. Christoph Wolff, whose magisterial biography of Bach bears the significant subtitle, 'The Learned Musician', says:

For Bach, art lay between the reality of the world – nature – and God, who ordered this reality…. 'What is art? An imitation of nature,' writes Bach's student Lorenz Christoph Mizler… It follows, then, that musical structure – harmonia, in the terminology of Bach's time – ultimately refers to the order of nature and to its divine cause.

But this imitation of nature differs from the Enlightenment idea. One of those who defended Bach, a professor of rhetoric at Leipzig University named Johann Abraham Birnbaum, wrote: 'Many things are delivered to us by nature in the most misshapen states', therefore art does not merely imitate nature but 'aids' it in order to 'improve its condition'. This echoes the climax of Luther's encomium to music in the preface to *Symphoniae jocundae*, a collection of Latin motets by early Renaissance composers, including his favourite, Josquin Desprez. After praising 'natural' music – the sounds of nature and the wonders of the human voice – Luther exclaimed: 'But when learning is added to all this, and artistic music, which corrects, develops, and refines the natural music, then at last it is possible to taste with wonder (yet not to comprehend) God's absolute and perfect wisdom in his wondrous work of music.' Far from disparaging learned music as 'artificially and laboriously fashioned' and neither 'pleasant nor moving' (Scheibe's words), Luther, and Bach after him, saw learning and labour as essential for achieving music's highest purposes.

Although the 1730s were a decade troubled by conflicts in Bach's professional life, they did not afflict his home life. His home was a happy,

This 19th-century painting by Toby E. Rosenthal depicts Bach and his family making music.

hospitable place. Carl Philipp Emanuel said it was like a 'dovecote, and just as full of life'. Bach enjoyed good conversation with relatives, friends, and colleagues. No doubt they enjoyed good food and drink along with it. (Bach also enjoyed his pipe.) And of course there was music-making, much of it by the immediate family. At the beginning of the decade Bach had written a letter to his friend Georg Erdmann in which he proudly and fondly said of his family that 'they are all born musicians, and I can assure you that I can already form an ensemble both vocally and instrumentally within my family, particularly since my present wife sings a good, clear soprano, and my eldest daughter, too, joins in not badly'. We have noted that by the end of the decade the older sons had attended university and started musical careers. And Bach was so confident that his youngest sons would follow suit that he included them along with their older musician brothers in the Genealogy of the Bach family musicians which he drew up in 1735 – even though Johann Christian was not yet one year old!

The mid- and late 1730s provided Bach and Anna Magdalena a respite from the deaths of their children. There were none between 1733 and 1739. After experiencing the deaths of seven children during the previous seven years, six years must have seemed like a long respite indeed. But the death in 1739 of twenty-four-year-old Johann Gottfried Bernhard, Maria Barbara's youngest living son, was tragic.

In 1735 Gottfried Bernhard had been appointed organist at St Mary's Church in Mühlhausen. Like his father's stay in Mühlhausen, his was brief – only sixteen months. He then applied for the town organist post at Sangerhausen, a post for which the town council had selected his father in 1702 only to have their selection overruled by the duke. Bach, in supporting his son's candidacy, even suggested that Sangerhausen owed him a favour because of what had happened some thirty-five years before. Gottfried was appointed and took up the post in February 1737, but the following spring he disappeared. No one knew where he was. From a letter Bach wrote to a friend in Sangerhausen it is clear that Gottfried had been a problem for some time. He refers to Gottfried as his 'misguided son', who had obviously been leading a dissolute life, borrowing money that he did not pay back. Bach had settled some of those accounts 'in the hope that he would now embark upon a new mode of life'. But now he has learned 'with greatest consternation, that he once more borrowed here and there and did not change his living in the slightest'. Bach concluded:

Since no admonition or even any loving care and assistance will suffice any more, I must bear my cross in patience and leave my unruly son to God's Mercy alone, doubting not that He will hear my sorrowful pleading and in the end will so work upon him, according to His Holy Will, that he will learn to acknowledge that the lesson is owing wholly and alone to Divine Goodness.

Gottfried resurfaced in January 1739, not in Sangerhausen but as a law student at Jena University. Four months later he died. We know nothing about the circumstances of his death except Gottfried Walther's report: that he died 'from a hot fever'.

Two chorales that are found frequently among Bach's works are 'Was Gott tut, dass ist wohlgetan' (What God does, that is rightly done') and 'Wer nur den lieben Gott lässt walten' ('If you but trust in God to guide you'). Their expression of trust in God must have given Bach much comfort and spiritual strength in the midst of sadness at home, frustrations at work, and a growing awareness that the religious and musical direction of the broader culture was turning sharply away from what he had inherited from his ancestors. Anna Magdalena drew her spiritual strength from the same wellsprings as her husband. Some of the pieces she added to her Notebook reveal the same trust. The first one is a chorale prelude on 'Wer nur den lieben Gott lässt walten', BWV 691. Among the other pieces she copied (and no doubt sang) are the chorale 'Schaff's mit mir, Gott', BWV 514:

> Deal with me, God, as you desire,
> To you my all is now disposed.
> You shall my needs bring satisfaction,
> As shall your wisdom it decide.
> You are my Father, you shall then
> Supply me, and that is my hope.
> (TR. AMBROSE. ALT.)

and the aria 'Warum betrübst du dich,' BWV 516, which resonates with the refrain of Psalm 42/3:

> Why are you so sad and bowed so prostrate to earth ...?
> If you do not rely upon God's will most firmly,
> You will in all of time discover no true repose.
> (TR. AMBROSE. ALT.)

The most explicit testimony to Bach's faith (if we exclude the witness of his

The only surviving book from Bach's personal library is a three-volume Bible with commentary called the 'Calov Bible'. The lower right-hand corner of this title page shows Bach's distinctive monogram and the date 1733.

music) is his copy of the three-volume edition of the so-called Calov Bible. His monogram in his distinctive handwriting is found on the title page with the date 1733, presumably the year of purchase. It is actually a Bible with commentary interspersed throughout the biblical text. Most of the commentary was selected by theologian Abraham Calov (1612–1686) from the writings of Luther. Occasionally Calov supplied his own commentary. The inventory of books in Bach's library that was drawn up after his death has the Calov Bible at the top of the list. The entire list contains fifty-two titles in more than eighty volumes. All the books are theological, including two sets of Luther's complete works. The three volumes of the Calov Bible are the only books from Bach's library known to survive today.

Bach did not just own the Calov Bible; he studied it. Corrections, underlining, and marginal notes in Bach's hand show that he knew Scripture well and read it carefully. He penned in well over 100 corrections. Some of them are from the erratum list at the end of volume III, but about 75 per cent are not on that list; Bach caught them himself, either from his own knowledge or by consulting another Bible. In about forty places he supplied missing words. Again, some may have been discovered because he had another Bible at hand, but he probably supplied some from memory, for example the missing words he inserted in Psalm 100:4: 'Give thanks to him and praise his name.'

Not surprisingly, some of Bach's underlining and marginal comments show his interest in the biblical foundations of church music. For example, at 1 Chronicles 25, a chapter that describes King David's provisions for the music of the tabernacle and for its 288 musicians, Bach wrote in the margin, 'NB. This chapter is the true foundation of all God-pleasing music.'

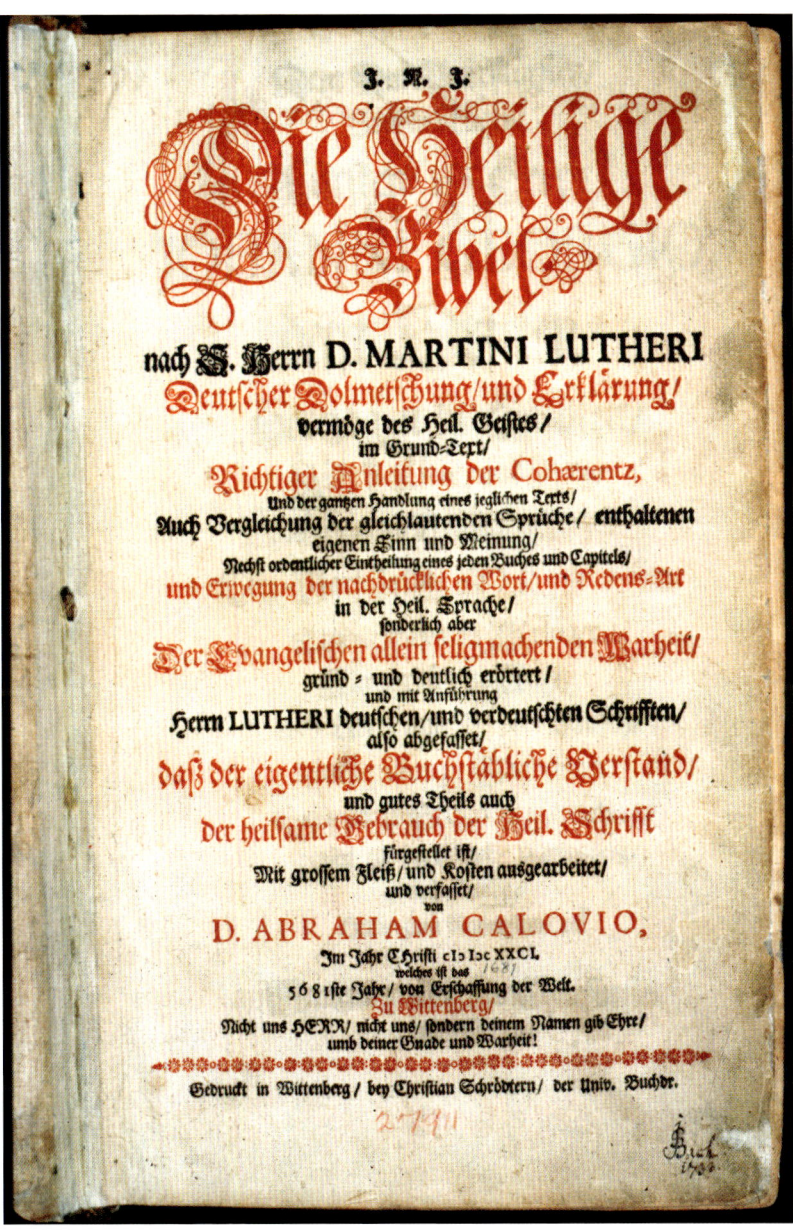

J. N. J.

Die Heilige Bibel

nach H. Herrn D. MARTINI LUTHERI
Deutscher Dolmetschung/ und Erklärung/
vermöge des Heil. Geistes/
im Grund-Text/
Richtiger Anleitung der Cohærentz,
Und der gantzen Handlung eines jeglichen Texts/
Auch Vergleichung der gleichlautenden Sprüche/ enthaltenen
eigenen Sinn und Meinung/
Nechst ordentlicher Eintheilung eines jeden Buches und Capitels/
und Erwegung der nachdrücklichen Wort/und Redens-Art
in der Heil. Sprache/
sonderlich aber
Der Evangelischen allein seligmachenden Warheit/
gründ- und deutlich erörtert/
und mit Anführung
Herrn LUTHERI deutschen/und verdeutschten Schrifften/
also abgefasset/
daß der eigentliche Buchstäbliche Verstand/
und gutes Theils auch
der heilsame Gebrauch der Heil. Schrifft
fürgestellet ist/
Mit grossem Fleiß/ und Kosten ausgearbeitet/
und verfasset/
von
D. ABRAHAM CALOVIO,
Im Jahr Christi cIɔIɔc XXCI.
welches ist das
568iste Jahr/ von Erschaffung der Welt.
Zu Wittenberg/
Nicht uns HERR/ nicht uns/ sondern deinem Namen gib Ehre/
umb deiner Gnade und Warheit!

Gedruckt in Wittenberg/ bey Christian Schrödtern/ der Univ. Buchdr.

The commentary on the first verse states that the duty of the tabernacle musicians was to 'express the Word of God in spiritual songs and psalms, sing them in the temple, and at the same time to play with instruments'. There are also suggestions that Bach identified himself and his vocation with the Old Testament temple musicians. For example, in Calov's preface to the Psalms he underlined the names of the three leading musicians in red ink – Asaph, Heman, and Jeduthun.

Perhaps more significant, especially in connection with Bach's problems with authorities and cultural trends as well as with the sorrows in his family, are the numerous underlines and *nota bene* markings in passages dealing with trusting God and submitting to his will. Some of them speak directly to carrying out the duties of one's office despite opposition.

If you are in an office and want to help and counsel matters, ingratitude will greet you and people will value little and forget your good deed, compensating good with wickedness, your great beneficence with idle thanklessness. If you are fainthearted, you will soon become annoyed and give up, but do not do so, hold firmly, persevere, carry out your office. God will be with you. [Bach marked 'NB' twice in the margin next to this passage.]

Others are more general; for example:

[Joshua 1] verse 5. No man shall stand to oppose you all the days of your life; as I was with Moses (with all my powerful support), so I will be with you: I will not fail you or forsake you (Deuteronomy 31:8. from which Paul takes consolation for all believers and applies to them this promise of God: I will not forsake or

neglect you. Hebrews 13: 5.) [Bach marked 'NB' next to 'I will not forsake you' both times.]

Therefore whoever wants to be a Christian and lead a godly life must learn to bear his own concerns and <u>to commend governance to God</u>, learning to say the 'Our Father': <u>Lord, Thy will be done</u>. [Bach's emphasis.]

This last quotation is from the commentary on Ecclesiastes 1:18. It might come as a surprise that the largest number of Bach's markings come from Ecclesiastes, a book so full of pessimism about the vanity of life. But the markings come in the commentary that constantly rings the changes on patient suffering and entrusting one's life to God. Here is the summary of Ecclesiastes as given by Calov. (Bach wrote 'Summa libri' ['summary of the book'] in the margin and emphasized the wording as shown.)

The Summa and the main point that Solomon speaks about and treats throughout his book is that there is no greater wisdom on earth under the sun than doing one's duty with devotion and the fear of God. Further, that we should not be fearful if things do not go the way we would like, but that we be satisfied and have God's will be done in all matters large and small. In Summa, that one be satisfied and content with whatever God provides, following the proverb: as God ordains, that will be my pleasure. And thus, let us <u>not trouble or consume ourselves with worry about what the future will or should bring, but rather remember that God has given me this office and work that I perform it willingly and with devotion, and that if my efforts and proposals do not turn out the way I hope, then may God's will and power prevail.</u>

Chapter 14

FINAL MONUMENTS: LEIPZIG (1739–1749)

Bach was fully aware that the Enlightenment was turning musical styles and ideals in a very different direction from what he had inherited from his ancestors and, more broadly, from the history of music since the Middle Ages. As we have seen, the Enlightenment extolled 'naturalness' and simplicity, viewed music as nothing more than an innocent pleasure, and therefore devalued music in education. Charles Burney (1726–1814) defined music as 'the art of pleasing, an innocent luxury, and a gratification of the sense of hearing'. Bach knew that that was the wave of the future, but he would never subscribe to such a low view of music however powerful the historical stream that carried it. The 'refreshment of spirit' that he mentioned on the title pages of his four *Clavier-Übung* publications was something higher than mere 'gratification of the sense of hearing'. And beyond refreshment of spirit he saw music as a powerful rhetorical art for conveying the truth of the Gospel. Overarching it all, he saw music as an art to glorify God. So his last decade was spent building monuments in sound to honour and memorialize the dying ideals – monuments that incorporate the gamut of styles, genres, forms, and techniques he had cultivated throughout his life. The monuments begin and end with works that are related to time-honoured liturgical and doctrinal texts. The first is the third volume of *Clavier-Übung*, a collection of organ works most of which are based on chorales; the last is the *B Minor Mass*.

In 1739 Bach published *Clavier-Übung III*, which has come to be known as the 'Catechism Chorales' or an 'Organ Mass'. Both titles are accurate but incomplete. The main contents of the collection are twenty-one chorale preludes, beginning with chorales derived from the *Missa brevis*, the Kyrie and the Gloria. There are two preludes based on each of the three Kyrie chorales, and three on the Gloria chorale, a total of nine (3 × 3), a Trinitarian symbol for those Trinitarian chorales. There is additional Trinitarian symbolism in the three Gloria preludes: all three are trios.

Following this 'Organ Mass' are the 'Catechism Chorales'. There are two preludes for each of six chorales related to the six sections of Luther's catechism: the Ten Commandments, the Apostles' Creed, the Lord's Prayer, Baptism, Confession, and the Lord's Supper. Each pair of preludes consists of a large one for full organ with pedals and a small one for manuals only. Thus the six large and six small pieces symbolize Luther's Large and Small Catechisms.

In addition to the chorale preludes, Bach included four duets and framed the whole collection with the Prelude and Fugue in E Flat Major, BWV 552, sometimes called 'St Anne' because the fugue happens to have the same opening notes as the hymn tune 'St Anne'. These additions resulted in more Trinitarian symbolism. The total number of pieces in the collection is twenty-seven (3 × 3 × 3). The framing prelude and fugue are in the key of E flat major (three flats). The prelude consists of three stylistically contrasting themes; the fugue has three subjects.

It is no coincidence that Bach published *Clavier-Übung III* in 1739. 1739 was the bicentennial of Leipzig becoming Lutheran. After the death of Saxony's Catholic duke, George the Bearded, Leipzig became Lutheran in 1539. Martin Luther heralded this event by preaching at St Thomas's Church on Whitsunday 1539. In August the same year, Leipzig officially accepted the Augsburg Confession. *Clavier-Übung III*, with its twenty-one preludes based on Reformation era chorales that relate directly to Luther's *Deutsche messe* (German Mass) and his catechisms, offered a most fitting homage to the great reformer in the bicentennial year.

In the autumn of 1739 Bach resumed the directorship of the *Collegium Musicum*, a post he had resigned in 1737. In November he and Anna Magdalena visited Weissenfels for a week. Such times away from Leipzig were not unusual. Their purpose was often business – examining a new organ, playing a recital, performing a cantata he had written for a special occasion such as a birthday. But sometimes they were for visits to family or friends. We do not know the reason for the Weissenfels visit. There were also trips to Halle the following spring and to Berlin in August 1741. Again we do not know the purpose of the visits. But we do know that the visit to Berlin was by Bach alone. Anna Magdalena stayed at home, perhaps because she was pregnant at the time. While Bach was away, she became seriously ill. Letters from home informed Bach that 'Frau Mama has been very ailing for a week' with 'violent throbbing of her pulse'. For a fortnight she did not have 'a single night with one hour's rest'. Family and friends feared she would die. The news must have given Bach distressing memories of Maria Barbara's death in Cöthen while he was away in Carlsbad. But Anna Magdalena recovered (albeit slowly), bore her last child, and lived on to see her youngest three children grow into adulthood.

During this time Bach must have been working on his set of variations that became known as the Goldberg Variations. He published it in 1741 as the fourth volume of *Clavier-Übung*. It was commissioned by a Count Keyserlingk, who had trouble sleeping. He asked Bach to write something to be played for him during his sleepless nights. According to Forkel, Keyserlingk liked the variations so much that he 'was never weary of hearing them'. He rewarded Bach with a golden goblet filled with 100 Louis d'ors. Handsome as that gift was, Forkel wrote that the worth of the variations 'would not have been paid if the present was a thousand times as great'. Posterity has supported Forkel's evaluation. Only Bach's own Chaconne in D Minor for solo violin (BWV 1004/V) and Beethoven's Diabelli Variations can rival it for first place among sets of variations.

The work got its popular name later. Johann Gottlieb Goldberg was a virtuoso harpsichordist who frequently played for Count Keyserlingk. But if it was he who played for Keyserlingk when the piece was published, it was quite a feat, because he was only fourteen at the time. But he was a prodigy, so it is possible.

The Goldberg Variations are not only Bach's monument to variation form; they also constitute a monument to the art of canon. Every third variation is a canon. The first canon is at the unison, and then in each successive canon the imitation is at a step higher until the interval of a ninth is reached in the twenty-seventh variation. For the thirtieth and final variation, Bach showed his sense of humor by writing a quodlibet (literally, 'whatever pleases') instead of the expected canon at the tenth. In it he wove two folk tunes into the harmonic pattern of the previous variations. Those who knew the tunes would have recalled the words:

> *I've not been with you for so long,*
> *Come closer, closer, closer.*

And:

> *Beets and spinach drove me far away,*
> *Had my mother cooked some meat,*
> *then I'd have stayed much longer.*

Perhaps Bach was recalling the family reunions described by Forkel, at which quodlibets were improvised by combining songs 'partly comic and partly naughty'. The singers 'laughed heartily,' wrote Forkel, and 'excited an equally hearty and irresistible laughter in everybody that heard them'. One hopes that a good laugh at the end of the piece helped the count get to sleep!

The baby Anna Magdalena was pregnant with during her recent illness was born in February 1742; she was named Regina Susanna and joined a household in which there were still six siblings: unmarried Catharina Dorothea (33), mentally deficient Gottfried Heinrich (18), Johann Christoph Friederich (9), Johann Christian (6), and Johanna Carolina (4). There would be no more children born after Regina Susanna, and neither would the parents again experience the death of one of their offspring. There would be two marriages – of Carl Philipp Emanuel in 1744, and, in 1749, of Elisabeth Juliana Friderica to one of her father's students, Johann Christoph Altnickol. These would bring four grandchildren into the family while Bach was still alive. The last of these was Elisabeth's son, named after his grandfather. He died in December 1749, having lived less than three months.

During his last decade Bach saw three sons and his son-in-law acquire music positions. In 1740 Carl Philipp Emanuel became the official court harpsichordist for King Frederick the Great. In 1746 Wilhelm Friedemann, after having a part-time post as organist in Dresden and losing out for another post, became organist at Our Lady's Church in Halle. In 1748 son-in-law Altnickol became organist in Naumberg, and in Bach's last year, Johann Christoph Friedrich was appointed court musician at Bückeburg. When eighteen-year-old Christoph Friedrich left home, Anna Magdalena gave him her personal Bible, stamped in gold with her initials, A. M. B. In it she wrote this inscription:

> As a personal memorial
> and for Christian edification
> A. M. Bach, neé Wulkin, presents
> this glorious Book to her dear son,
> Your loyal and affectionate Mamma.

Activity in Bach's household slowed down during his last decade, and occasions for joy outnumbered occasions for sorrow. Professional activity also slowed down. Bach continued his teaching and music duties at St Thomas's and St Nicholas's, but he used prefects as much as possible to help with the teaching; and since he rarely performed new compositions in the churches, preparation for performance was more routine. He continued to accept private students and examine organs, but he gave up the directorship of the *Collegium Musicum* early in the decade. All in all there was more time left to devote to composition.

Between the 'bookends' of the monuments of the last decade, *Clavier-Übung III* and the *B Minor Mass*, Bach focused his attention on the two most intricate and uncompromising musical forms, canon and fugue. The publication of the Goldberg Variations in 1741 did not spell the end of his canon-writing. A few

years later he added fourteen canons to his personal copy of the 'Goldbergs'. Then in 1747 he became a member of the Society of Musical Sciences founded by his former student Lorenz Christoph Mizler. He was the fourteenth member to join. (Fourteen is the number symbol of his name. See above, Chapter 9, and note the fourteens yet to come.) For admission to the society, he submitted a triple canon, BWV 1076, and Canonic Variations on 'Von Himmel hoch', ('From heaven on high'), BWV 769. He also had his portrait painted; in it he is holding the triple canon.

During the 1730s Bach had been working on a second volume of the *Well-Tempered Clavier*, BWV 870–893, which like the first is a collection of twenty-four preludes and fugues, one in every major and minor key. He compiled a manuscript of the collection between 1739 and 1742, but he continued to work on it. His pupil and future son-in-law, Johann Christoph Altnickol, made a complete copy of the revised work in 1744, to which Bach continued to make minor revisions.

A second monument to fugal writing, *The Art of Fugue*, BWV 1080, overlapped with his work on the *Well-Tempered Clavier II*. An early version

Pages from the score of *The Art of the Fugue*, the early version of which was completed in 1742.

consisting of fourteen pieces, twelve fugues and two canons, was completed around 1742. Later he added two more fugues (making fourteen in all) and two more canons. Bach died before he could see the work through to publication. In 1751 son Carl oversaw the publication, but the final fugue was incomplete; an annotation by Carl says that Bach died while working on the last fugue. What makes Carl's remark all the more poignant, is that the fugue breaks off just after Bach had introduced a new theme that spells his name – B A C H (in German notation B = B flat and H = B natural). A popular story that Bach died while composing the final fugue grew out of this. But in all probability Bach had finished the work, or at least sketched its ending. But by the time Carl brought it to publication, the page containing the end of the last fugue had been lost. Carl's note was a romantic fiction.

Another monument to fugal and canonic compositions grew out of Bach's visit to King Frederick the Great in his palace at Potsdam (just outside Berlin) in 1747. Frederick was a music-lover, and Bach's son Carl was his harpsichordist. Bach had been in Berlin in 1741 but had no opportunity to visit the king, who was at the time involved in the First Silesian War. The Second Silesian War, which included the Siege of Leipzig in 1745, also prevented a visit. Bach could not even go to Berlin to attend the baptism of his first grandson. But in 1747 the opportunity finally came, probably with Carl making the arrangements. The opportunity to see his grandson must have been as enticing to Bach as a visit to the king. Bach and Wilhelm Friedemann left Leipzig and travelled by coach to Potsdam some ninety miles away. They arrived on Sunday 7 May. In the evening, with little or no time to rest and freshen up after the long journey, they were taken to the palace at the time when the king held regular chamber music sessions

FINAL MONUMENTS: LEIPZIG (1739–1749)

featuring himself playing flute. When Frederick was informed of Bach's presence, 'His August self', as a news report has it, 'immediately gave orders that Bach be admitted'. According to Forkel, Frederick announced: 'Gentlemen, old Bach is here.'

The main item on Frederick's agenda was to hear Bach improvise – more specifically to improvise a three-part fugue on a theme the king himself had written. According to the newspapers, Bach executed the task so well that 'His Majesty was pleased to show his satisfaction' and all present were astonished. Later the king asked for another improvisation on his theme, this time a six-part fugue, a feat so difficult that Douglas Hofstadter compared it to playing 'sixty simultaneous blindfold games of chess, and winning them all'. It is not clear whether Bach used the king's theme or deferred because of its unsuitability for the task. But, whether using the king's theme or another, he did improvise a six-part fugue 'to the pleasure of His Majesty and to the general admiration'. Despite the amazement of all who heard, Bach himself was not satisfied. He went home and composed thirteen pieces, all (including a six-part fugue) based on the king's theme. He sent them to the king, and called the collection a *Musical Offering* (BWV 1079).

Frederick never acknowledged receipt of Bach's offering. It is doubtful that he paid it any attention. If he did, he would have been mightily put off by Bach's music, for even though he was reported to have been pleased with Bach's performance at Potsdam, what interested him was not Bach's music but his improvisatory skill. For Frederick, Bach's performance was akin to a circus act – or as Samuel Johnson might have said, to a dog walking on two legs.

Bach and Frederick were about as far apart as two eighteenth-century European men could be. Bach was sixty-two, twice married, father of twenty

Frederick the Great's palace
'Sanssouci', just outside
Berlin. Although it was
completed in 1747 just
before Bach's visit, the palace
where he played for Frederick
was the city palace, which
was destroyed by fire during
World War II.

children, a devoted Lutheran, and thoroughly German middle class. Frederick was thirty-five, married only for political expediency, childless, vehemently anti-Christian though religiously tolerant with regard to his politics, and culturally a 'frenchified' aristocrat. Musically, Frederick's taste ran to the lighter *galant* styles favoured by the Enlightenment. For him music was merely a diversion, an escape from the business of life. Frederick had a special loathing for canons and fugues. He said they 'smelled of the church'. Bach and Frederick were worlds apart. Their meeting was a clash between Bach's old world of faith and Frederick's new world of 'enlightenment'.

So what kind of music did Bach dedicate to him? Two fugues, one in three parts, one in six; a trio sonata; and ten canons. Even though Frederick hated fugues, it made sense to include the fugues because they were what he had asked Bach to improvise. Even so Bach did a couple of things that seem designed to tease Frederick. First, he filled the three-part fugue with *galant* features but treated them in a very un-*galant* way. Second, he called the fugues by their older generic name, ricercare. Thus he highlighted the ancestry of a genre that Frederick scorned as old-fashioned.

Including a trio sonata also made sense because sonatas were common fare at Frederick's musical soirées, and this one included a flute, Frederick's

This 19th-century engraving based on a painting by Herman Kaulbach, depicts Bach playing for Frederick the Great.

instrument. But again Bach teased Frederick. The trio sonata he wrote is a four-movement *sonata da chiesa* (church sonata) instead of a three movement *sonata da camera* (chamber sonata), the only kind that Frederick would tolerate for his evenings of musical diversion. This sonata is too difficult to play merely for relaxation. If Frederick tried to play it, he would have had to focus on it as intently as he did on his battle plans and political schemes during the day.

But worst of all – for Frederick – were the canons, the most regimented of all musical forms. Both the name (canon meant 'rule', 'law') and the form (one part strictly imitating another part) make it clear why Bach often used canons to symbolize law, or more specifically the Ten Commandments. And here he presents this irreligious, canon-hating king with *ten* canons.

Michael Marissen has noticed other aspects of the collection that suggest there is more to it than appears on the surface. The dedication contains language with theological overtones that not only give off a generalized 'smell of the church' but also resonate more specifically with the theology expressed in the opening chorus of the *St John Passion*, which is addressed to Jesus as the 'Lord' whose glory is seen 'in the deepest lowliness'. Particularly interesting in regard to the theological overtones in the preface is the fourth canon. It is a canon in augmentation, that is, the notes are 'augmented' to be twice their normal length. It carries the inscription, 'As the notes increase [in length], so may the fortune of the King.' The style of the piece is that of a French overture, a style associated with royal pomp and splendour. But an interesting thing happens when the notes are lengthened. They become very slow and the music loses its pomp and splendour. Instead it becomes quite melancholy, especially when

coupled with Frederick's chromatic melody. As Marissen puts it, 'The strikingly melancholy *Affekt* and the "de-regalized" canonic solution link regal fortune (worldly works, glory) not to splendour, might, and fame, but to the theology of the Cross' which recognizes Jesus' glory in his 'deepest lowliness'.

Of course such interpretations, however plausible, are speculative. But two things are clear. First, even aside from theological readings, the *Musical Offering* stands against Frederick's 'enlightened' views about music and upholds the views of Bach and his ancestors. It would not be surprising, then, if Bach also incorporated various symbols and procedures that could be 'read' as standing theologically over against Frederick's 'enlightened' unbelief. Second, there is nothing in such readings that Bach had not said explicitly and repeatedly in the cantatas, motets, Passions, and oratorios, and would say one last time in his final monument, the *B Minor Mass*.

Sometime in the late 1740s, Bach, probably realizing that his end was near, began to put together the work we call the *B Minor Mass*. As with *Clavier-Übung III*, he turned his attention to time-honoured liturgical texts – this time reaching back beyond Luther to five texts in Latin, the 'universal' language of the church. The five texts were texts that had been sung daily in the Mass since early Christian times: the Kyrie ('Lord, have mercy'), the Gloria ('Glory to God in the highest'), the Credo ('I believe'), the Sanctus ('Holy, holy, holy'), and the Agnus Dei ('Lamb of God').

The B Minor Mass *was the culmination
of his life's work. It is a lasting
monument to the venerable art that
went into its making, and to the highest
purposes to which music can aspire.*

Bach started with the *Missa brevis* (i.e., the Kyrie and Gloria) he had written in 1733 and sent to the elector along with his petition for a title. To expand that into a *Missa tota* (full Mass) he needed to add the Credo, Sanctus, and Agnus Dei. For some parts of those texts he found earlier compositions that would work as parodies; for the rest he composed new music. The final compilation brought together music that nearly spans his career, from 'Crucifixus' ('He was crucified'), which is a parody of a movement from a cantata he wrote in 1714 in Weimar, to a movement like 'Confiteor' ('I confess'), which he composed in 1748–1749. More broadly it spans the centuries. It not only employs the high Baroque style but also reaches back to the Renaissance in its *stile antico* (old style) movements and forward at times to the new *galant* styles. He even reached back to the Middle Ages by using Gregorian chant in the 'Credo' and 'Confiteor' movements.

Besides its chronological and stylistic inclusiveness, the *B Minor Mass* exhibits a panoply of compositional techniques. But in the *B Minor Mass*, unlike in his instrumental monuments, he could do more than summarize various styles, genres, and compositional techniques, and bring them to their culmination. He could also put the whole range of his musical-rhetorical skills to work on the words to which most of his great predecessors since the late Middle Ages had devoted their utmost compositional skill, and with which Christians had prayed and confessed their faith over the centuries.

Bach knew that the times were changing and that he and his art were being left behind. The *B Minor Mass* was the culmination of his life's work. It is a lasting monument to the venerable art that went into its making, and to the highest purposes to which music can aspire.

Chapter 15

DEATH: LEIPZIG (1750)

Bach was blessed with a robust constitution. With the exception of his final illness, we know of only one occurrence of ill health. A fever in 1729 prevented him from going to Halle to visit Handel. (An earlier attempt to visit Handel had also failed; the two would never meet.) But in the spring of 1749, for reasons unknown, his health deteriorated rapidly. Early in the year he had still been active. As late as 4 April he had performed the *St John Passion*, and later in the month he was still consulting with an organ-builder. He even became embroiled in another controversy over the importance of music in education.

In May 1749, Johann Gottlieb Biedermann, a rector in Freiberg, published a pamphlet attacking music as a disreputable activity that had ill effects on human character. He warned students against joining 'Jubal's brood!' (Jubal was 'the father of all those who play the lyre and pipe', according to Genesis 4:20–21.) Bach could not ignore such an attack on the art he had cultivated so assiduously throughout his life, especially when it came from the rector of a school. But failing health prevented his direct involvement. So he persuaded a colleague to write a rejoinder. Bach liked what he wrote and it was published. Exactly what transpired in the aftermath is unclear. What is clear is that Bach, almost on his deathbed, took another strong stand against the Enlightenment's trivialization of music. To the end of his life, regardless of the strength of the cultural current that was flowing in another direction, he swam strenuously upstream, upholding the musical and theological ideals of his ancestors.

Sometime before June a report that Bach was ill circulated widely enough that on 2 June the Saxon prime minister, Count Heinrich von Brühl, sent a letter to Leipzig councillor Jacob Born recommending that they audition Gottlob Harrer for Bach's position upon his 'eventual decease'. We do not know the nature or severity of Bach's health problem at the time, except that his already poor eyesight was deteriorating. So we do not know how imminent his death seemed or how urgent was the need to look for his successor. But already on Wednesday 8 June, Harrer performed his trial cantata in the Three Swans concert hall. The rapid response to Count Brühl's letter and the performance on Wednesday in a concert hall instead of in a church in a Sunday worship service suggest secrecy and perhaps an eagerness to be done with Bach.

But Bach did not oblige; he lived on for more than a year. Whatever his illness was in the late spring, by late summer and early autumn he was healthy enough to mount two performances that seem calculated to show that he was not finished yet. The first was on 25 August, when he performed Cantata 29 again for the change of town council. If he played the virtuosic organ part himself, it would have offered an especially vivid demonstration that he was not standing, as the opening line of Cantata 156 puts it, 'with one foot in the grave'. The other performance showed that he had not lost his readiness to champion traditional musical values over against Enlightenment lightness and simplicity. It was a performance of a secular cantata, BWV 201, commonly known as 'The Contest between Phoebus and Pan'. The contest between the two mythological characters is a musical one in which Phoebus represents the tradition of serious, learned music, while Pan represents the lighter styles favoured by the Enlightenment. Momus and Mercury are objective judges; Midas and Tmolus champion Pan and Phoebus respectively. Phoebus wins, and Midas, for his support of Pan, is given ass's ears! But he has his consolation – popular support. As Momus tells him, 'You have brothers like yourself. Lack of judgment and folly now want to be neighbours with wisdom.'

In late 1749 and early 1750, Bach had his two oldest sons perform their own compositions in Leipzig. Wilhelm Friedemann performed a cantata on 30 November, the First Sunday of Advent, and Carl Philipp Emanuel performed his Magnificat on one of the Marian feasts, either Purification (2 February) or Annunciation (25 March). It looks like Bach was telling the town council that his sons were more qualified to replace him than Harrer was, but that might be reading too much into the events. Perhaps he was just getting relief from duties that were becoming increasingly difficult for him to perform. In any case, it would not be long before a successor would be needed.

In March Bach's eye problems became much worse and he suffered considerable pain. But a famous English eye doctor, John Taylor, was in Leipzig lecturing at the university. Bach arranged to have him operate on his eyes. On 1 April the newspapers reported that the operation had taken place and was successful. On 4 April they were still reporting success, not only for Bach but for two other men, a doctor and a merchant, who were operated on by Taylor. But within a day or two, Bach needed a second surgery. It was unsuccessful; his blindness persisted and the medication rendered him almost continuously ill, though not so much as to keep him from accepting a new student as late as 4 May. Then on 18 July he experienced a surprising recovery, during which he could see for a brief time. But this was followed by a stroke and a high fever. Two of Leipzig's best doctors were called in, but

to no avail. On 22 July, at home, Bach received his final communion.

There is a story that the blind Bach dictated a chorale prelude on his deathbed. The 'deathbed chorale' bears the appropriate title 'Vor deinen Thron' ('Before your throne'), BWV 668. The story, however, cannot be true, because the piece in question is known to have been composed much earlier. In fact there are two earlier versions. The earliest version goes back to the *Orgelbüchlein* where it has the title 'Wenn wir in höchsten Nöten sein' ('When we are in greatest need'), BWV 641. Probably around 1740 Bach greatly expanded the original version, and later yet he made a third version that differs only in a few details from the second version, and it bears the new title, 'Vor deinen Thron'. Christoph Wolff plausibly suggests that Bach, thinking about his impending end during his last days, recalled the piece he had composed earlier and asked a friend to play it for him on his pedal harpsichord. After hearing it Bach thought of some minor improvements and dictated them to his friend. He also recalled another text that was sung to the same tune as 'Wenn wir in höchsten Nöten sein' and had his friend

Bach on stained glass
window in St Thomas's
Church in Leipzig.

retitle the piece 'Vor deinen Thron'. Its words made a most fitting prayer as
death came near:

> *Before your throne I herewith tread,*
> *O God, and humbly ask that you*
> *not turn your gracious face from me,*
> *a poor sinner.*

On the evening of 27 July 1750, Bach went before God's throne. According to
the Obituary he did so 'quietly and peacefully, by the merit of his Redeemer'.

There is no reason to suspect that the authors of the Obituary were
mollifying the truth with their report that Bach died peacefully. All his
life Bach had faced the deaths of those nearest and dearest – his parents,
siblings, children, and first wife, not to mention other relatives and friends.
But already as a child he had learned that death need bring no terror to one
who puts his trust in 'the merit of his Redeemer'. From one of his school
textbooks, a compendium of theology by Leonard Hutter, he had learned
the answer to this question:

*Q. What consolation can believers oppose to the terrors of death, which of all
evils, is the most terrible?*

*A. The pious, who believe in Christ, know that death is not death to them, but on
the contrary, a gate and entry to life.*

Throughout his career Bach wrote sublimely beautiful and comforting cantatas dealing with death – BWV 106 in Mühlhausen, 161 in Weimar, and 125 and 82 in Leipzig, to mention just a few. The basis for their comforting message is the theology in Hutter's answer in the compendium. That answer in turn resonates with the final words of the Nicene Creed: 'I confess one baptism for the forgiveness of sins, and I look for the resurrection of the dead, and the life of the world to come.' Bach's setting of those words in the *B Minor Mass* reveals a profound understanding of the theology involved.

Bach set the two halves of the text, 'Confiteor ...' ('I confess ...') and 'Et expecto ...' ('I look for ...'), in two different but connected movements. At the end of the 'Confiteor' movement, something unexpected happens. Instead of coming to a normal ending, the music slows down, turns sharply in a different tonal direction, and comes to a pause on a half-cadence in an unexpected key. Then in a series of chords wandering slowly in mysterious directions the words of the 'Et expecto' phrase are sung – 'and I look for the resurrection of the dead'. The slow, mysterious chord progressions seem to be at odds with these joyful words. The words, not to mention musical expectations, call for a lively celebratory chorus with trumpets and tympani. That will come; Bach will not disappoint. But for the moment the music creates a sense of awe and wonder. It invites the listener to pause and contemplate the incredible mystery that is being confessed: 'I look for the resurrection of the dead.' The apostle Paul said: 'Behold! I tell you a mystery' (1 Corinthians 15:51–52). Bach, through his music, seems to be saying:

Listen, we confess a mystery: 'We shall not all sleep, but we shall all be changed, in a moment, in the twinkling of an eye, at the last trumpet. For the trumpet will sound, the dead will be raised imperishable, and we shall be changed.' Now stop for the moment. Ponder with awe and wonder this incomprehensible mystery!

After the contemplation comes the celebration. The harmonies take focus, the tempo quickens, and the trumpets sound. In ascending fanfares and running sequences the orchestra and choir joyfully celebrate resurrection and life as they repeat and complete the sentence: 'I look for the resurrection of the dead and the life of the world to come. Amen.'

But there is still more to the theological depth of this music. The slow, mysterious section that connects the two movements underscores the connection that the Creed makes between baptism and resurrection: 'I confess one baptism ... and I look for the resurrection of the dead ...' The connection has its basis in Romans 6:4, words that Bach knew from Luther's Small Catechism even before he had studied Hutter's compendium: 'Thus we indeed are buried with him through baptism into death, so that, as Christ was raised from the dead by the glory of the Father, we too might walk in newness of life.' In baptism the believer dies and rises with Christ. Bach made that clear by means of musical parallels. The two contrasting settings of 'Et expecto' ('I look for the resurrection of the dead') bear a striking resemblance to the earlier choruses about Christ's death and resurrection, 'Crucifixus' ('He was crucified') and 'Et resurrexit' ('And he was raised'). With those parallel pairs of choruses, Bach linked the believer's death and resurrection to Christ's. 'Death', as he learned as a child, 'is not death to them, but ... a gate and entry to life.'

Chapter 16
EPILOGUE

Bach's reputation among his contemporaries was not what we would expect today. He was widely recognized as an organist without peer, but as a composer he was considered old-fashioned, out of step with the 'enlightened' time in which he was living. His incredible mastery of counterpoint was acknowledged but not valued. So when he died, his music almost died with him.

Almost, but not quite. Carl and Friedemann continued to perform their father's works, as did his students. A few others kept his music alive among small circles of aficionados. One of these, Baron Gottfried van Swieten, introduced Mozart and Beethoven to Bach's works. In a letter Mozart mentioned that Swieten had loaned him some of Bach's music. When he played Bach's fugues for his wife Constanza, he wrote that she scolded him for not writing fugues, 'the most intricate and beautiful kind of music'. A few years later Mozart heard the St Thomas choir perform Bach's motet for double chorus, 'Singet dem Herr ein neues Lied' ('Sing to the Lord a new song'), BWV 225. An eyewitness account tells us:

Hardly had the choir sung a few measures when Mozart sat up, startled; a few measures more and he called out, 'What is this?' And now his whole soul seemed to be in his ears. When the singing was finished he cried out, full of joy, 'Now there is something one can learn from!'

Mozart's reaction was not unique. Beethoven, who by the age of twelve had played most of *The Well-Tempered Clavier*, called Bach the 'father of harmony' and punned that his name should not be *Bach* ('brook') but *Meer* ('sea'). Ever since Mendelssohn performed the *St Matthew Passion* in 1829,

*Today, more than halfway
into the third century after his
death, Bach's music is loved
around the world.*

the first performance since Bach's lifetime, all the great composers have paid him homage. In an address given at a commemoration of the 200th anniversary of Bach's death in 1950, Paul Hindemith said that Bach 'climbed the highest rung of artistic production attainable by mankind'. In his music, he said, 'We have beheld the summit. It is a symbol for everything noble towards which we strive.' Not many would accuse Hindemith of being excessive in his praise.

Accolades for Bach's music come not only from other musicians. On hearing Bach, Goethe remarked that it was 'as if the eternal harmony were conversing with itself, as it may have done in the bosom of God just before the Creation of the world. So likewise did it move in my inmost soul.' Closer to our own time, when Nobel Prize-winning novelist Halldor Laxness was asked what one book he would take to a desert island, he said, '*The Well-Tempered Clavier*. It contains everything.' The scientist Lewis Thomas, when asked about what music to send into outer space in order to communicate with whatever intelligent life might be out there, said, 'I would vote for Bach, all of Bach, streamed out into space, over and over again. We would be bragging, of course, but it is surely excusable to put the best possible face on at the beginning of such an acquaintance.' As it turned out, the 'Golden Record' sent into space on *Voyager 1* and *2* in 1977 has as its first item the first movement of the Brandenburg Concerto No. 2. It also contains a movement from the Partita for Solo Violin in E Major and the Prelude and Fugue in C Major from *The Well-Tempered Clavier II*, making Bach the only composer to be represented in outer space with three pieces.

Today, more than halfway into the third century after his death, Bach's music is loved around the world. Concerts, festivals, conferences, and recording projects proliferate. As I write, two sets of his complete works are available on CD. Three projects to record all of his 200 plus cantatas are complete, and another is well on its way to completion. And of course there are thousands of recordings of individual works and collections. One reviewer recently asked, 'Why all this Bach?' He answered simply, 'Because Bach, of all composers, is the one whose complete works are most nourishing.' But most who praise Bach are not content to leave it at that. As pianist and composer Scott Foglesong notes, 'A reverential tone is common when people talk about Bach. The scent of transcendence perfumes all discussion.'

The extraordinary quality that posterity has heard in Bach's music makes a stark contrast not only with how most of his contemporaries heard it but also with the ordinariness of Bach's life. It has often been said that his life was not very interesting. To be sure his life was not glamorous or full of exciting adventure or plagued by huge emotional crises. In many ways it was decidedly middle class. He went to school, learned the family trade, entered the job market, worked hard, married, and supported his large family, mostly within a small geographic area that was hardly at the hub of European culture and musical life. Had G. K. Chesterton written a biography of Bach, he might have written an apology similar to the one he wrote for himself: 'I am sorry if the landscape or the people appear disappointingly respectable and deficient in all those unpleasant qualities that make a biography really popular.'

At the end of a lecture on the *St Matthew Passion*, Leonard Bernstein nicely caught the contrast between Bach's ordinary life and his extraordinary work. Holding up the score of that monumental work, he exclaimed:

And think that this is only one work in the vast catalogue of Bach's output, one volume among all these dozens: songs, dances, suites, partitas, sonatas, toccatas, preludes, fugues, cantatas, oratorios, masses, passions, fantasias, concertos, chorales, variations, motets, passacaglias – the white-hot creation of fifty ceaseless years.

And what is it that holds these pages together? The religious spirit. Every note was dedicated to God ...

This is the spine of Bach's work: simple faith. Otherwise, how he could have turned out all that glorious stuff to order, meeting deadlines, and carrying on so many simultaneous activities? He played the organ, directed the choir, taught school, instructed his army of children, attended board meetings, kept his eye out for better paying jobs. Bach was a man, after all, not a god.

Bach no doubt would agree; he would claim no more than that he was a man of simple faith who dedicated his work to God. However, when Bernstein added 'but he was a man of God, and his godliness informs his music', Bach would demur – not at being called a man of God, but at the idea that his own godliness is at the heart of his music. He would claim no godliness of his own. He would claim only what Luther called 'alien righteousness', the righteousness imputed to him through the sacrifice, the death on the cross, of Jesus Christ. So he would hope that his God, not his godliness, informed his music. He believed, as a chorale says, that 'in Adam's fall we all fell'. But he also believed the words of another chorale, the basis for one of his greatest cantatas, BWV 4:

Christ Jesus lay in death's strong bands,
for our offences given;
He is again arisen
and brings us life from heaven.
Therefore let us joyful be
and sing to God right thankfully
loud songs of alleluia!
Alleluia!

(TR. RICHARD MASSIE, ALT.)

With that reason to sing, Bach would say, along with the great English poet George Herbert:

... with my utmost art
I will sing thee,
And the cream of all my heart
I will bring thee.

For Further Reading

Sources

The New Bach Reader, ed. Hans T. David and Arthur Mendel, rev. Christoph Wolff (Norton, 1998). A substantial selection of the most important source material in English translation.

Reference

Oxford Composer Companions: J. S. Bach, ed. Malcolm Boyd (Oxford University Press, 1999). Short entries on people, places, genres, instruments, technical terms, and more; also longer articles on major works and important topics. Comprehensive and authoritative.

Biographies

James R. Gaines, *Evening in the Palace of Reason* (Fourth Estate, 2005). Interweaves the biographies of Bach and Frederick the Great, culminating in their meeting in 1747.

Christoph Wolff, *Johann Sebastian Bach: The Learned Musician* (Norton, 2000). The definitive biography. Up to date and rich in detail.

Special studies

The Calov Bible of J. S. Bach, ed. Howard H. Cox (UMI Research Press, 1985).

Alfred Dürr, *The Cantatas of J. S. Bach* (Oxford University Press, 2005).

Mary Dalton Greer, 'From the House of Aaron to the House of Johann Sebastian', in Gregory G. Butler et al., eds., *About Bach* (University of Illinois, 2008).

Robin A. Leaver, *J. S. Bach and Scripture* (Concordia, 1985).

Michael Marissen, 'The Theological Character of J. S. Bach's *Musical Offering*', in D. R. Melamed, ed., *Bach Studies* vol. II (Cambridge University Press, 1995).

Jaroslav Pelikan, *Bach Among the Theologians* (Wift and Stock, 2003).

Calvin R. Stapert, *My Only Comfort: Death, Deliverance, and Discipleship in the Music of Bach* (Eerdmans, 2000).

Günther Stiller, *Johann Sebastian Bach and Liturgical Life in Leipzig* (Concordia, 1984).

Glossary

aria A solo vocal composition within a larger piece such as a cantata, oratorio, or Passion. It is usually accompanied by basso continuo and one or more obbligato instruments. It is lyrical in style and often virtuosic with lots of repetition of words and phrases. (Compare **recitative**.)

basso continuo A type of instrumental accompaniment that is almost ubiquitous in Baroque music. It consists of a bass line played by a bass instrument (cello, bassoon, etc.) and a chord-playing instrument (harpsichord, organ, lute, etc.) whose player improvises the harmonies above the bass line.

canon A type of composition in which one or more parts imitate the leading part throughout. The imitation can be at different pitch levels (at the unison, at a fifth, etc.) and at different time intervals (after one beat, after one measure, etc.). A round is a simple type of canon at the unison that can be endlessly repeated.

cantata In the Baroque period this term usually referred to vocal chamber music. Although Bach rarely used the term, it has become the standard designation for his multi-movement compositions for choir, vocal soloists, and orchestra. Most of his cantatas are sacred, but he also wrote some for secular occasions such as the birthday of a duke.

cappelle The vocal and instrumental musical ensemble of a court.

chorale Congregational hymns of the Lutheran church, typically referring to those that originated during the Reformation and early post-Reformation eras. Pieces commonly referred to today as 'Bach chorales' are Bach's four-part harmonizations of those melodies; the melodies themselves are not by Bach.

chorale prelude An organ piece based on a chorale melody.

concerto A multi-movement instrumental composition that pits a solo instrument (in a solo concerto) or small group of instruments (in a concerto grosso) against the full orchestra.

continuo See **basso continuo**.

figural music Music, usually quite elaborate, for voices and instruments, as opposed to simpler choral music with no more than continuo accompaniment.

fugue (adj. fugal) A type of composition based on a theme (called the subject). The piece typically begins an exposition in which the subject is presented in imitation in all the parts. Throughout the rest of the piece the subject will appear periodically in different parts, sometimes overlapping. Bach was unrivalled in his mastery of highly sophisticated fugal techniques.

galant A term that refers to the simpler, fashionable musical styles of the Enlightenment.

Missa A musical setting of the Ordinary of the Mass, i.e., the texts that appear in every Mass as opposed to the Proper texts which change according to the day. A *Missa tota* is a setting the Kyrie, Gloria, Credo, Sanctus, and Agnus Dei texts. A *Missa brevis* is a setting of just the Kyrie and Gloria.

motet A sacred choral composition without obbligato instruments.

obbligato instruments   Instruments that have essential, independent parts, i.e., parts that do not simply double voices.

oboe da caccia   A Baroque oboe pitched a fifth lower than the oboe.

oboe d'amore   A Baroque oboe pitched a third lower than the oboe.

ostinato   A melodic phrase that is constantly repeated throughout a piece or section of music, most typically in the bass part.

partita   See **suite**.

piccolo cello   A small cello tuned a fifth higher than the regular cello.

polyphony (adj. polyphonic)   Music in which all the parts are more or less equal in melodic and rhythmic importance, as opposed to music in which one part has the primary melody and the others are accompanimental.

recitative   A solo vocal composition within a larger piece such as a cantata, oratorio, or Passion. Some (called secco recitatives) have only a continuo accompaniment; others (called accompanied recitatives) include additional instruments. The style is declamatory – words are not usually repeated, there is usually just one note per syllable, and the rhythms and melodic inflections are close to those of oratorical speaking. (Compare **aria**.)

recorder   An end-blown '(whistle)' flute that had not yet been entirely replaced by the cross-blown flute in Bach's time.

stile antico   Baroque music that more or less imitated the older Renaissance style. Typically associated with ecclesiastical rather than theatrical or chamber styles.

sonata   A multi-movement composition for one or more solo instruments, usually with continuo accompaniment.

suite   A multi-movement instrumental composition in which all or most of the movements are based on the rhythmic style of dances such as allemande, minuet, gavotte, etc.

toccata   Single-movement but highly sectional keyboard works. They typically begin with an improvisatory section followed by a series of sections in alternating fugal and non-fugal styles.

viol   See **viola da gamba**.

viola da gamba   Literally 'leg viol'. A bowed stringed instrument of various sizes with six or seven strings, played in an upright position, resting on or between the legs. In Bach's time it had not yet been entirely replaced by the instruments of the violin family.

violone   Various sizes of large viols tuned below the normal bass viol. The predecessor of the modern double bass.

An Overview of the Surviving Compositions of J. S. Bach

Sacred vocal music

About 200 church cantatas

2 Passions (*St Matthew* and *St John*)

3 oratorios (Christmas, Easter, Ascension)

6 motets

1 Magnificat (two versions)

4 *Missae breves*

B Minor Mass

About 250 harmonizations of chorales and sacred songs

Secular vocal music

About 20 secular cantatas

Organ music

About 200 chorale-based works

About 30 non-chorale-based works (preludes and fugues, etc.)

6 trio sonatas

6 concerto arrangements

Harpsichord music

15 Two-part Inventions

15 Sinfonias (three-part inventions)

6 *French Suites*

6 *English Suites*

6 *Partitas*

The Well-Tempered Clavier I and *II* (48 preludes and fugues)

Italian Concerto

Overture in the French Style

Goldberg Variations

16 concerto arrangements

7 toccatas

About 60 suites, preludes, fugues, fantasias, capriccios, etc.

Instrumental (non-keyboard) music

6 Sonatas and Partitas for solo violin

6 Suites for solo cello

6 works for solo lute

About 12 sonatas for violin or flute with continuo or obbligato harpsichord

6 Brandenburg Concertos

2 violin concertos

1 concerto for two violins

1 concerto for flute and violin

14 concertos for 1, 2, 3, or 4 harpsichords

4 orchestral suites

Canons and late contrapuntal studies

Canonic Variations on 'Von Himmel hoch'

7 miscellaneous canons

14 canons added to the manuscript of the Goldberg Variations

A Musical Offering

The Art of Fugue

Index

Picture
Acknowledgments

akg images: pp. 151, 158, 167

Alamy: pp. 12, 19, 33, 44, 51 CuboImages srl; p. 28 Richard Wareham Fotographie; pp. 35, 164 imagebroker; pp. 36, 132, 141 INTERFOTO Pressebildagentur; p. 40 Christopher Gannon; p. 46 Arco Images GmbH; p. 67 Pat Behnke; p. 77 Bildarchiv Monheim GmbH; p. 96 World History Archive; p. 101 The Print Collector; p. 123 PHOTOBYTE, pp. 137, 146, 172 Lebrecht Music and Arts Photo Library, p. 138 Mary Evans Picture Library

The Art Archive: pp. 70, 107 Bach House Leipzig / Alfredo Dagli Orti; pp. 88, 139 Bach House, Eisenach / Alfredo Dagli Orti

The Bridgeman Art Library: p. 56 Zentralbibliothek, Weimar, Germany; pp. 81, 128, 160 Staatsbibliothek, Berlin, Germany; USA; p. 99 Thomaskirche, Leipzig, Germany, p. 163 Newberry Library, Chicago, Illinois

Corbis: p. 11 Jan-Peter Kasper/dpa; pp. 16, 27, 95 The Art Archive; p. 62 Stefano Bianchetti; p. 179 Hulton-Deutsch Collection

Getty: p. 11 Imagno/Austrian Archives

Klassik Stiftung Weimar: p. 68 Weimarer Schlosskirche, Christian Richter (1557–1667), Klassik Stiftung Weimar, Museen, GR 1230

Photographers Direct: pp. 93, 136 Lebrecht Music & Arts

Scala: pp. 14 (2007), 15 (2006), 58 (2009), 89 (2005), 113 (2005) © Photo Scala, Florence/BPK, Bildagentur fuer Kunst, Kultur und Geschichte, Berlin

Topfoto: p. 3 The Granger Collection / Topfoto

Lion Hudson

Commissioning editor: Kate Kirkpatrick

Project editor: Miranda Powell

Designer: Nicholas Rous

Picture researcher: Jenny Ward

Production manager: Kylie Ord